The Awkward Spot

The Awkward Spot

Getting Things To Grow in Impossible Places

Daphne Ledward

 Robson Books

Colour photographs by John Hands
Line drawings by Chris Olney

First published in Great Britain in 1989 by Robson Books Ltd,
Bolsover House, 5–6 Clipstone Street, London W1P 7EB.

British Library Cataloguing in Publication Data

Ledward, Daphne
    The awkward spot.
    I. Title
    635
ISBN 0 86051 558 3

Typeset by Bookworm Typesetting Ltd
Printed In Great Britain by St Edmundsbury Press Ltd, Bury
St Edmunds, Suffolk.

Contents

Acknowledgements   6

Introduction   7

Damp shade   18

Dry shade   36

Hot, arid places   51

Moist, sunny areas   71

Areas of very shallow soil   78

North- and east-facing walls and fences   86

The narrow passage   101

Salt-affected areas   113

Vandal-affected areas   125

Postscript   140

Useful Addresses and Bibliography   141

Acknowledgements

I would like to thank Johnson's Seeds of Boston, Lincolnshire, and Notcutts Garden Centre, Peterborough, for allowing me the freedom of their trial and display grounds.

Introduction

What's an awkward spot?

Looking back over my gardening life, I think I have only once been defeated as far as getting something to grow reasonably well regardless of position was concerned. I knew it was a gamble, but I was desperately short of space. At the time I was living in a cottage which, over the years, had lost nearly all its garden to building plots. What was left was what the estate agent's brochure euphemistically described as a 'patio garden'.

The position was a long thin strip of dark, sour earth between our property and the one next door, which was thatched. As is customary with most thatched roofs, there was no gutter and so all the rainwater from that side of the roof, which was quite sizeable, ran off in copious yellow torrents every time there was a shower. The level of light between the properties was minimal as our eaves had a considerable overhang, next door was three storey high, and a 6-foot (2-metre) high wall had been built at the end of the strip in an attempt to minimize the amount of litter hurled over by the users of the bus-stop on the other side. Added to that, the piece of ground, although over 30 feet (9 metres) long, was a mere 3 feet (1 metre) wide, so the dice were well loaded against successful cultivation from the outset.

'So why on earth', you are asking yourself, 'would anyone who is supposed to know a bit about gardening be so stupid as to attempt to grow anything in such a spot?' In my defence I would ask you to consider how an inveterate planter feels when confronted with an area the size of a postage-stamp after years of having a plot of reasonable extent. Having already filled the garden to overflowing, there was still bare soil to be had in this strip, and it had to be exploited at all costs if I were not to die of horticultural boredom.

I decided upon a low, ground-cover planting, and chose three species I felt were virtually indestructible: *Cotoneaster dammeri*, *Vinca major* (the common greater periwinkle) and *Rubus tricolor*, a rambling form of blackberry. They did not look particularly good, partly because of the sober leaf coloration and partly because they did not enjoy their all-too-regular dousings with thatch-water. For my elderly dalmatian dog the area had a magnetic attraction as a loo.

Altogether the scheme was not an unqualified success, but it takes a lot to defeat Daphne, and I was only finally persuaded to abandon it when the builders arrived to point the stonework of the house next door. Even happy, healthy plants would have turned up their leaves at the treatment they received from reinforced toe-caps and mortar droppings. Mine were neither happy nor healthy, and it did not take much for them to succumb. I was finally beaten, and regretfully gravelled the strip. Now that is what I call an *impossible* spot!

This kind of situation apart, however, there are few areas which cannot be planted successfully, though judging by the number of queries I receive about so-called problem areas, most garden-owners have at least one area they find a struggle.

The first thing which has to be remembered is that not all plants like the same conditions, and if you try to knock a square peg into a round hole, so to speak, then you will have a problem and the awkward spot will be one of your own making. For example, if you try to grow shade-lovers in a hot, sunny position, they are going to take exception; similarly, if you plant species requiring full sun in a cool, damp, shady place, they will not do much, either. It is essential, therefore, not to buy on impulse, or to set your heart on a particular thing, unless you are sure you can give it a happy home. Take advice or check in a good plant encyclopaedia first (see Bibliography). This simple step eliminates a good half of what could be difficult areas.

Not-so-Awkward Spots

High altitude gardens
I have often seen high altitude areas – those around 1000 feet (300 metres) or more above sea-level – described as problem spots, and yet some of the most beautiful British gardens are situated high up.

Admittedly, the height of the area does have a bearing on what can be grown, but not as much as one might think. For every 600 feet (180 metres) increase in altitude, the average annual temperature decreases by 2°F (1°C) and the start of the growing season is put back by three days. Rainfall and wind increase and solar energy falls, so it is obvious that the plants to choose would be different from those you would consider in, say, south and west coastal districts, but there are still many subjects which, apart from being slightly slower to establish and not growing quite as rampantly, would be perfectly suitable.

Windy areas
Again, if one has a problem in a windy garden, it is generally self-made, usually by wanting to run before you can crawl. There are many shrubs which will stand up to strong winds quite successfully, for example willow, poplar, alder, mountain ash and whitebeam, hawthorn, and conifers like pine and spruce. These can be planted as a 'first line of defence' - they are quick-growing but can be pruned back and so in a very short time will provide shelter for other, more exacting plants in their lee.

Of course, if you have a very small, windy garden, shelter planting may not be practical, but the problem can still be overcome satisfactorily. Even a low fence will make a windbreak, but if you do not like the thought of this, or if the deeds of the property prohibit it, you can provide a temporary netting windbreak, or choose low-growing subjects which will offer less wind resistance: dwarf shrubs, dwarf conifers, heathers and alpine plants should cause little trouble. Remember, too, that wind is unlikely to be a problem to a well-maintained lawn and, in my opinion, if grass will grow well, the position will not be all that daunting.

Seaside gardens
Seaside gardens in themselves should not pose a problem − in fact, they offer much easier growing conditions than those inland as the differential between highest and lowest temperatures is much less, making the plants more unlikely to suffer from frost damage. Before moving to my present property, I lived on the north Lincolnshire coast, not renowned for its ease of cultivation, though famous for being 'so bracing'! As far as plant hardiness was concerned, I found much less difficulty in growing dubious subjects like phormiums, helichrysums, hebes and agapanthus than in my previous garden, which was another 20 miles (32 km) further inland as the crow flies.

It is interesting to note that people living in the areas to the immediate west of Newcastle upon Tyne have less trouble growing many plants than those living in Herefordshire, although the latter is much further south. The reason for this is that the sea which is so close to Newcastle keeps the temperature higher in winter, while in summer it keeps it cooler, making the plants grown locally tougher and more resistant to cold periods. Herefordshire, on the other hand, is so far inland as not to receive benefit from the sea either to the east or the west, and I have experienced amazingly low temperatures when working in that county.

The real problems with maritime areas are wind and salt spray. Wind on its own can be tackled as I have already described. Salt spray is much more serious. The right sort of shelter-belt planting, using subjects which are both wind- and salt-resistant and dense enough to absorb most of the spray, like *hippophae* (sea buckthorn), *Populus alba* (white poplar), and *Pinus maritima* (Corsican pine) will help, but this is not always practicable, which is why I have devoted a section to maritime planting later, on pages 113–124. A whole new maritime-type environment is being created these days with the use of salt on roads in winter to prevent ice forming.

The other point that must be remembered in connection with seaside planting is that, as with every other situation, you are going to encounter different conditions depending on the locality of the maritime area. For example, the climate of the west coast is influenced by the Gulf Stream, making it easier to grow many plants on the north-west coast of Scotland than on the south-easterly coastline of Kent.

New gardens on building sites
These are often classed as problem areas – and undoubtedly most of them are. If you are lucky, the builders will have left the site compacted and littered with brick-bats, wall-ties and empty cement bags. There will be hard, grey craters where the concrete mixer was washed out, and deep ruts everywhere. If you are unlucky, you will have the same thing, only covered with a thin smear of camouflaging topsoil. At least with the former situation, you know exactly what you are getting. When a cover-up job has been done, you will not know how bad things are until your lawn goes critical and your plants start to look poorly. I have included this type of problem here only to make suggestions as to how it can be overcome, since it is a situation that can be remedied once and for all, without having to resort to looking for special plants.

My most important advice to people who find themselves faced with the headache just described is not to take anything at face value

– even if it was a feature of the builder's advertisement that the garden would be left ready for cultivation – his ideas and yours might not coincide! If you know your patch is filled with builders' rubble then you have got some hard work ahead of you. Before you can consider planting anything, you must dig the area thoroughly, breaking up any compacted areas and removing as much of the rubbish as you can. You should add any organic material you can get your hands on – farmyard manure, spent mushroom compost, spent hops, garden compost or peat – to improve the soil texture, and if you are dubious about whether there is any decent topsoil on the plot, it might be wise to buy in a load, providing you are certain it is of good quality.

If the builder has done a cover-up and you are not sure what is below, the best thing is to dig a few deepish holes around the garden. If the digging is easy and you do not strike a brick-mine, the chances are the site was well cleaned up. However, if you encounter a hard layer a few inches or centimetres down and a lot of buried debris, you can be highly suspicious and, regrettably, you could be in for even more hard work – digging the whole piece of ground over deeply to break up hard soil and removing as much rubbish as you can, as this will only become a problem in the future.

Once done, however, your difficult situation no longer exists, and you are free to go ahead and plant up as you wish – remembering, of course, that there may be other awkward areas which are not quite so readily remedied!

The garden on clay
If you are wrestling with hard, yellow clods as you read this, I know you will not believe me when I say that clay soils are some of the best for producing healthy plants. Clay, because it is not free-draining, retains nutrients far longer than most soils, making the ground extremely fertile and more economical when it comes to applying fertilizers. In addition, it provides a firm, stable anchorage for taller plants, reducing wind-rock and its attendant root damage. Against this is the fact that, because the particles are so small and so close together, it is difficult for sufficient air to enter the soil to keep it sweet, with the result that clay is often acid. Furthermore, it tends to be a cold soil, especially where drainage is bad, and it is slow to warm up in spring.

The way to tackle a clay soil is to understand its structure, and try to do something about it in the plants' favour. The object of improvement is to loosen the soil so that air can enter; incorporating plenty of organic material, such as farmyard manure or, especially, spent mushroom compost, which contains lime in addition to horse manure, is helpful, as is sharp (not soft) builders' sand (this is obtainable from builders' merchants, but you should check to make sure it really is sharp sand; the kind used in making mortar will not open the soil up sufficiently as the particles are not angular enough). There are several products which claim to deal with a clay soil and these are usually successful if applied in sufficient quantities, but they are expensive and you can get the same results by applying horticultural gypsum and peat.

A clay soil will grow most common plants, especially roses, quite successfully, before years of cultivation have turned it into a 'friable loam'. The main problems occur through waterlogging in winter, and the surface drying out rock-hard in summer. If you know your soil is prone to waterlogging, you should choose plants specially suited to that environment, which are described on pages 18–35 (for shady spots) and pages 71–77 (for open areas).

In the early days of cultivation, it may be wise to steer clear of alpine-type plants, which only do well in a sharp, free-draining soil, or grow them in specially constructed raised beds or rockeries, otherwise their roots are liable to rot.

Cracking in hot weather can be prevented by applying a mulch of peat, bark or similar material to a well-dampened surface in spring; this will also help to improve the soil structure as it is gradually incorporated into the ground through cultivation and the action of worms.

If a clay soil is properly looked after, there should be no reason, subject to the climate of the area, why a wide range of plants should not be grown with great success.

Sandy soil

Sandy soil is more difficult to grow things in successfully than clay, because sand is so free-draining that it is permanently dry unless copious amounts of water are given, and regular fertilizing is essential. However, in its favour is the fact that it is unlikely to become waterlogged for long enough to cause permanent root damage, even in really wet weather. So long as much organic matter of any sort is dug in every time the soil is turned over, which will help to conserve moisture, and mulching is applied to the damp surface in spring, one should be able to achieve very good results.

Just how successful one can be when growing on a sandy soil can be shown by my own example. Always on the look-out for new bits of ground in different areas and of differing types, I recently took over a plot about 20 feet (6 metres) long and 17 feet (5 metres) wide, composed of almost pure sand, in an extremely dry area near Norwich. I had been assured by the owner that it was totally impossible to grow anything on it, and I like a challenge. When I looked at it, the weeds were waist-high, which gave me some hope. If weeds would grow, so would other things. The main drawback was that this south-facing, totally enclosed piece of ground had no water supply, so whatever was planted would have to take its own chance.

I had access to an inexpensive supply of seed potatoes, and decided that this would be a good subject with which to clean up the plot. I dug in vast quantities of compost, imported from my own garden, and several bales of peat. I also top-dressed with Arthur Bower's potato fertilizer and felt I could do no more. The early potatoes were planted during the last week in March, and the main crop two weeks later. I was able to harvest no less than 2 cwt (100 kg) of potatoes, perfect apart from some scab. Throughout the growing season they had received no artificial watering; what natural water there was had been retained in the organic matter dug in before planting. Which all goes to show that one person's opinion of an impossible spot and another's can be totally different!

The soil-less garden
This is a most unusual situation, but, again, one that exists, because it existed for me. Also, it is not a hopeless case.

I have already described in the introduction how I, an obsessive gardener, found myself faced with a postage stamp. Although it was force of circumstances which landed me in such a spot, the more off-putting a situation appears, the more I feel inclined to tackle it. However, this particular garden was especially unprepossessing. In addition to the strip which beat me, it had a badly laid patio about 8 feet (2.5 metres) square, and the remainder comprised a very large garage – ideal for storing my tools and the decrepit Mini truck and trailer which were my bread-and-butter in those days – and an oddly shaped bit about (on average) 25 feet by 16 feet (7.5 metres by 5 metres). It was broader than long, which is always difficult to plan, and it faced north, although it did receive oblique east and west sunshine in summer.

Another problem was the existence of a right-of-way across a shared drive, which, although we did not realize it when we purchased the property, was to cause more problems than all the rest put together, as the owner of the right-of-way, who lived in a property built on what used to be part of our cottage's garden, was keen to stick to the letter of the law, which is that the right-of-way must only be used for access: one cannot loiter thereon. This made it very difficult when we discovered that the garden, such as it was, had originally been part of a public house car-park, and consisted of nothing more than hoggin and gravel. A faint heart would have paved it, but not so Daphne, who wanted the biggest growing area possible. To do this entailed digging out all the rubble and carting it across a busy road, as we were not allowed to position our skip on the right-of-way outside the back gate.

After removing enough rubbish to fill two large skips, the level had been reduced by 2 feet (0.6 metre). A more accessible site could have then been replenished with good topsoil, but everything had to be brought in in manageable quantities. However, nothing in this vein is impossible to a keen gardener, and an excellent substitute for garden soil was made by bagging up the dredgings of a local dyke and spreading it, to which was added bales of moss peat, old growing bags, some very juicy pig manure from a farmer client, and a top dressing of Vitax Q4 fertilizer. There was very little suitable stuff that wouldn't grow on this improvised soil – the problem was that most of it grew too well! I pass this 'impossible' garden regularly and, ten years on, it still looks good.

The tiny garden
Many people class very small gardens as awkward, but to me they are a delight. Every plant can be made to mean something individually and a well-stocked garden need not break the bank. You will naturally have to choose the species carefully; space will not allow for big, rampant growers, but most plants have a dwarf, prostrate, slow-growing or fastigiate (upright) form and, with the specialist

nurseries abounding in this field these days because the average garden is getting smaller, you should be able to find the things you want without trouble. If you lead a busy life, it is much more pleasurable to sit back in a tiny, well-maintained garden and regard your efforts with pride than to suffer acutely from conscience as the weeds grow up around you.

The real awkward spot

So what does constitute a difficult growing area? I suppose it can be defined as a place where you need to have more than a nodding acquaintance with plants in order to choose varieties which will not only survive, but will thrive and look first-rate. Shaded areas spring immediately to mind, but not all shade is particularly difficult providing you have a working knowledge of plants. The ordinary shade cast by buildings is no real worry – there are thousands of plants which will do well under such conditions. But add dampness and soggy soil and your choice is narrowed down considerably. Or look at the shade under a dense canopy of branches, or under the eaves of a house, where most natural water is excluded. These are the places where you could end up thinking that no plants exist which would survive in such inhospitable spots.

The vast majority of plants will flourish in sunny places. But if that sunny area should be excessively hot and dry, many will take exception. Or if they have their roots constantly submerged in water, they have to be designed to survive such conditions, otherwise they will gradually rot.

There are dozens of climbers available to adorn a south or west wall, which is sunny. But try planting some of these against a cold north or east wall, and they will not be quite so keen. Not many plants appreciate a draughty position, and yet all over the country there are narrow passages between houses – virtually useless pieces of ground which turn a terraced house into a more desirable 'semi' or a semi into an 'executive detached'. I often wonder how much more usable ground would be available if property owners were not quite so snobbish about the type of home they lived in. After all, some of the most architecturally pleasing residences are in terraces, and they do not have problems with draughty strips of ground between buildings, hardly large enough to put a ladder up for maintenance. However, these strips exist and there are many people, like me, who hate seeing pieces of earth unused. There are plants which are happy under such conditions, so a section of this book will be dedicated to them.

Some areas of soil are so shallow you would think nothing would grow in them. But leave them alone, and see how quickly they become weed-ridden. If weeds will grow, the area can be put to a much more useful purpose.

I have already mentioned areas affected by salt. It is a sorry sight these days to drive along a main road at the end of winter and see the devastation caused by salt spray after gritting to minimize icy road surfaces, and yet as I drive around the country, I still see people planting expensive hedges which, come the first winter, will not stand an earthly chance. Even well-established shrubberies and hedges are dying off as the residual salt in the soil increases. Road-side gardens are gradually taking on the conditions of sand dunes, and this should be borne in mind when planting them up.

Then there are the areas which fight a losing battle against vandals. Not all 'vandals' come with two legs – many of them have four, and they are much more difficult to deal with. A bored teenager can be quite 'chicken' when confronted by a wall of sturdy, 1-inch (2-cm) spines, but if it is a meal for a passing rabbit or deer, the offender is not quite so likely to be discouraged.

These, then, to me are the awkward spots – those that, if you do not get it right, are likely to look a mess. But for every situation there is sure to be something which will fit the bill – it might not be the 'special' plant you hoped you could grow, but it could look just as attractive if it is thriving.

No matter where the problem area is, the plants put into it will only give of their best if they are given every care and consideration. Just because the spot might be the 'poor man' of the garden, it is no excuse to skimp the preparation of the ground, planting, and subsequent after-care. Thorough digging is essential, and so is soil improvement as described on page 12. In the majority of areas, plants will benefit from their roots being surrounded by a 'planting mix' of a mixture of good garden soil, peat, and sharp sand. This provides a good medium for plants to root into, which will encourage quick establishment. The only exception is when planting into very heavy, wet soil; unless you are using plants which revel in such conditions, you run the risk of creating a 'sump' if you backfill the planting hole with a much lighter mixture, which can cause root rotting. If it is totally impossible to improve a heavy area throughout, it is better to backfill with more or less the same soil, perhaps just adding a little peat or well-rotted manure. It may take longer to re-establish the plants, but the chances of survival are much greater.

As with all plants, their subsequent success depends very much on how they are looked after. Watering will be necessary in dry spells, and mulching is beneficial: it conserves moisture and as the mulch breaks down it supplies small amounts of nutrients. A top dressing of bonemeal in autumn can be useful, especially on poor or shallow soils, and a spring dressing of a balanced fertilizer like Vitax Q4 will keep the plants growing strongly. Where plants are not growing under the most ideal of conditions, you may find they can become the target of insect attack. If you notice any distortion of the young leaves, holes, or nibbled edges, a spray with a general purpose insecticide containing pirimicarb (which is harmless to bees and ladybirds), permethrin, pyrethrum or malathion will check the damage. Similarly, plants under some form of stress are more prone to fungal diseases. The most likely of these is powdery mildew, which appears as a powdery white deposit on the youngest leaves. This can be controlled with Benlate, thiophanate-methyl, propiconazole or carbendazim.

Bearing the foregoing in mind, what now remains is to consider the area you are struggling with, and ask yourself what the factor is that has caused so much trouble in the past. You may not be able to change this, but from the plant suggestions on the following pages you may find just the things to fill your awkward spot and help you to achieve a good display at last.

Damp shade

Damp shady areas are found where buildings, trees or other tall structures are situated where they obscure direct sunshine for most, or all, of the day, and where the soil is naturally badly drained, or is constantly receiving water running off another area, for example, at the bottom of a slope or around a drain-pipe. Damp shade does not usually occur immediately under trees or against buildings or walls, as these tend to prevent rain-water reaching the ground in that spot.

There are two ways of tackling a garden, or part of it, which is damp and shady. The first is to try to remedy the causes, either by removing the object causing the shade, or by installing what could turn out to be quite an elaborate and complicated land drainage system, or by channelling any run-off from buildings into a soakaway. These remedial measures are rarely, if ever, practical, however. It may not be all that difficult to take the storm-water off a roof into a soakaway, even though to do this requires both a certain amount of energy and some knowledge of what you are doing to achieve total success, but you can hardly demolish your home, or that of your neighbour, if it happens to block much of the sunshine from reaching your garden in summer, and all of it in winter. Nor would it be a good idea to start felling mature trees some distance away purely for the sake of sunlight, even if it were possible and legal to do so.

If the trees happen to be in your garden and there is no preservation order on them, you could consider whether they were good specimens, contributing to the overall landscape, or whether they just happened to be there because nobody had thought to do anything about them. If you do decide that they should remain, and again assuming that there is no order on them preventing pruning or similar work, there are ways in which you could let more light into the garden. Maybe the bottom branches could be removed to admit low sunshine to enter below the crown, or perhaps careful thinning of the branch structure might be possible, which could turn dense shade into dappled sunlight, enabling a much wider range of plants to be grown.

Some slower-growing hardwoods, like beech, respond well to an overall tipping back and shaping of the outer growth, and a very few – for example, the upright forms of willow – 'pollard' satisfactorily (that is, the branches emerging at the top of the trunk are cut back hard periodically). If this is done on a regular basis, the stature of the tree is kept much smaller so that it will not cast such long shadows and a larger area of the garden will be able to receive sun sometime during the day.

I cannot stress strongly enough, however, that the person performing the work must have a good comprehension of the trees and what he or she is doing, otherwise it will be not so much surgery as butchery. Furthermore, if there is any doubt about whether or not the local authority will allow such work to be done, do check with the council first. Even if there is an order on the tree or trees, you may still be allowed to carry out shaping, or other remedial work, providing the local authorities are informed in advance of what you intend to do and they approve of it. It may even be that you will only be allowed to carry out the work if you use a tree surgeon approved by them, which could involve you in a lot of money.

While on the subject of money, the same comment applies if you decide to do something about the wet conditions of your soil. It is usually possible to install land drains to dispose of the excess water, but here again you have to know quite a bit about the geology of your area and the principles of land drainage if it is to work. It is not just a question of digging trenches and putting drainage pipes at the bottom – you must have an accurate herringbone layout across the whole area, and plenty of ballast at the base, otherwise the pipes will just clog up. And, of course, the water has to go somewhere (preferably not under your neighbour's fence!). If you do not feel up to doing the job yourself, there are excellent drainage experts who would do the work for you, but at a price.

The easy alternative to all this hassle is not to fight the situation, but to adjust to it. It is quite possible to have a delightful garden which is both very damp and very shady if you select your plants with care. Damp and shade are not an easy combination of circumstances to deal with, and there are many plants which will not do well. This could be why many people begin to despair and feel that damp shade is an impossible medium to grow anything in successfully, but this is not the case!

Before I begin to describe the subjects which positively revel in such adversity, I ought to mention the kinds of things you are wasting both time and money to try and grow. To start with, unless you cannot live without it, you can forget about growing a good lawn. There are mixtures available based on woodland grasses which do quite well if the soil is good and reasonably free draining, but where the ground is constantly damp and the surface is compacted (a frequent result of regular mowing), you will soon begin to develop all sorts of problems, like mosses, algae (a black or dark green slime) and liverworts. Although there are chemicals which will deal with these on a temporary basis, they will return at low light levels unless the drainage is improved.

The alternative to grass is often paving, but unless you really need a hard-standing, I would be inclined to think twice about this also, as in dense shade it will green over quickly and unless you make a habit of washing it, preferably with an algacide, it could well become a serious safety hazard.

Failure of bulbs and similar plants sporting fleshy underground parts like tubers, corms and rhizomes is commonly caused by planting in unsuitable soil conditions, and dampness is definitely one of these. Most bulbs will rot if they are constantly waterlogged. Daffodils, crocuses, bluebells, lilies, bearded irises or whatever need some sunlight to build up a good food-storage organ for the following year, and a reasonably moist (but not wet) soil to keep them growing strongly before the leaves die back. If they receive no sunlight at all, and the bulb is deprived of oxygen in the soil because of the water content, they will quickly deteriorate. First the flowering will become affected, fewer being produced each year, then the plants will vanish completely as the bulb rots away.

Tulips, especially, which originated in much warmer, drier climates than the British, will not put up with anything other than a warm, well-drained spot. Similarly, most summer-flowering species, like ixias, gladioli and sparaxis must have good growing conditions to last more than a season, regardless of whether they are lifted annually and stored correctly or not.

The only bulbous plant you may feel it is worth trying is erythronium. The two forms most widely available are *erythronium dens-canis*, the dog's-tooth violet, and *E. tuolumnense* 'Pagoda'. This is by no means an easy subject, as it prefers light shade and an acid soil, but I have known it grow happily in full shade if the soil is moist, but not heavy, with a pH of 5–6, and plenty of organic matter is present. The dog's-tooth violet has a flower resembling a true violet (of which it is no relation), but with attractively spotted leaves like a smoother, smaller version of pulmonaria. *E. tuolumnense* 'Pagoda' is taller and yellow, and the flowers are distinctly lily-like.

Annuals (plants which flower, seed and die over a period of twelve months) rely entirely for propagation on the masses of seed they produce, and this usually ripens better and is more viable if it matures in full sun. Therefore it is unlikely that, given their own choice, annuals would pick a damp, shady place to make their home; even the

Dog's-tooth violet

odd 'stray' that has a go in this kind of position will grow badly and produce little good seed, ensuring that the species does not make a habit of that sort of thing. You will only be disappointed if you try to grow things like pot marigolds, larkspur, love-in-a-mist, clary, night scented stocks, linaria, nemophylla, godetia and cornflowers; while you are wasting your money if you buy most bedding plants – salvias, antirrhinums, petunias, tagetes and ageratums, for instance – for such a spot, as they will not flower well.

There may be, of course, a place in your garden where for some reason it is not convenient to plant anything other than temporary subjects. If this is the case, there are three varieties of bedding plants – not annuals, but perennials cultivated as annuals – which you might like to chance. *Begonia semperflorens*, the fibrous-rooted begonia, is easily obtainable as plants in late spring and early summer from garden centres, nurseries and garden shops selling summer bedding. The most popular variety is F_1 (first generation) hybrid 'Organdy Mixed', with a wide colour range from white to red, and green or bronze foliage. There are many varieties available from seed companies in single colours, however, such as 'Olympia White', 'Thousand Wonders' in red, white or rose, 'Sheila' (orange-scarlet) and 'Rosanova' (cerise-pink). These are all F_1 hybrid varieties and, because they are hand-pollinated to produce uniform seed and subsequent habit, they are likely to be expensive. Fibrous-rooted begonias are not easy to grow from seed as they are prone to damping-off, but I have had great success with F_1 'Pink Avalanche' – strong-growing, large plants where one packet gives an enormous number of healthy seedlings, even if sown in an unheated greenhouse in April.

Busy lizzies (impatiens) were grown as houseplants for many years before their bedding potential was recognized. Their success in the home depended to a large extent on the fact that they need a lot of water, so it was difficult to kill them off through over-indulgence with the watering can. Similarly, although they will not rot if planted in very moist soil, if light levels are low neither will they flower as profusely, but instead are inclined to develop a great deal of lush top growth. The F_1 hybrid 'Accent' series is perhaps the most universally found and can be obtained in pink, red, rose, salmon and white, or for mixed colours on compact plants, look for F_1 'Elfin Mixed'. Busy lizzies can be grown from seed in exactly the same way as other bedding plants if you have a heated greenhouse or light windowsill in the home, but it can be tricky to get the watering right after germination – too much or too little and they turn up their petals.

The third summer bedding plant you could look out for is mimulus, the monkey flower. This is perhaps better known as a perennial pondside plant, but breeding has produced some attractive hybrids with large and interestingly coloured flowers. Again, if the position is completely sunless, you will not find the same profusion of flowers as in a moist and sunny or partially shaded position, but you will get some colour. If you like mixed colours, try 'Extra Choice Mixed' or F_1 'Calypso'. If you are buying them as bedding plants, you may be restricted to an assortment of shades, but if you want to grow your own, and this can be done in exactly the same way as with busy lizzies, there is an attractive yellow form called F_1 'Viva'. 'Queen's Prize Strain' is particularly interesting, as the flowers are spotted and mottled in a whole range of colours.

While on the subject of bedding, so often an area which looks good in summer is really dull in winter when the plants have been removed. If you intend to bed-up a shaded, wet area in summer, it can be replanted in the autumn with polyanthus and *Primula wanda* hybrids. Providing the ground is not heavy clay or completely waterlogged, these should flower pretty well the following spring.

Shaded areas, to look really eye-catching, need to rely heavily on leaf colour, form and texture. Plants flowering in dark areas do not in general sport colourful blooms, and as a general rule subjects with bright flowers do not thrive in dark areas. This, then, excludes many of the favourite shrubs like hypericum, forsythia, lilac, deutzia, philadelphus, weigela and so on, also roses and flowering herbaceous border subjects like lupins, delphiniums, Michaelmas daisies, lychnis, geums, erigerons, heleniums and coreopsis. All of these will become diseased, straggly and flowerless, if indeed they survive at all. When planting up dark areas one also has to be careful with variegated-leaved varieties; some retain their variegation well, even without any sun at all, but many will lose their brightness and look very lack-lustre.

Plants which revel in wet situations have specially adapted roots which enable them to get the most from the moisture in the soil and tolerate well the lack of air between the particles. While there are very few plants which will survive with no water at all (in temperate regions, at any rate) there is a difference between adequate amounts of moisture and waterlogging. Plants enjoying the former conditions will eventually rot off at the roots in the latter, therefore those to be planted in areas which are both sunless and soggy have to be a bit special, even though their appearance might be otherwise.

The best effects are therefore obtained by not trying to fight the problem, but to go with it as far as the choice of plants is concerned, grouping them so there is the maximum contrast in form and texture – for example, large-leaved plants near spiky or feathery ones, pale green against dark green, maximum use of suitable variegated plants, and so on.

It goes without saying that, in difficult areas of this nature, plants must be given the best possible conditions available in which to grow. Thorough digging and the addition of plenty of organic material, and sharp sand if the soil is heavy, will work wonders. Wet soils do not lose their nutrients through leaching in the same way as light sandy soils, so if the site is reasonably rich in plant foods in the first place (through the incorporation of manure and a top dressing of a balanced or compound fertilizer like growmore or Vitax Q4 at planting time), it might be all that is necessary for several years. Too much feeding can be as bad as – or worse than – too little.

Don't forget that, as with all other things in life, there are degrees of circumstance: moist conditions ranging from damp to soggy, shade from a light dappling to really dark. Plants which like one degree might not necessarily like another, for example heavy shade instead of light shade, very moist instead of slightly moist. The following pages contain my selection of plants which grow well in various kinds of shade and dampness. I have indicated the optimum conditions for each; to achieve the maximum success it is advisable to stick to these recommendations, though most plants have a margin of tolerance.

Hardy herbaceous perennials

I have memories of the most well-known member of the aruncus family, **Aruncus sylvester**, romping happily in a damp spot behind my aunt's house when I was a child. The plant saw no sun – though it would perhaps have performed better if it had received a little. It is a tall plant, growing up to 6 feet (2 metres) high with plumes of white flowers in June and July. There are two smaller forms, A. plumosus 'Glasnevin' and A. sylvester 'Kneiffi', which has attractive dark foliage.

Similar in flower form and leaf shape are **astilbe** and **filipendula**. Astilbes make good marginal plants for water gardens, but will flower well in shade provided it is not too dense. There are many varieties available, with colours ranging from deep red to pure white, and heights from 1 foot (30 cm) to 4 feet (120 cm). Of particular note are *A.* × *arendsii* 'Bressingham Beauty' (pink), 'Fanal' (a strong red), 'Snowdrift' (white), and *A. chinensis pumila*, a shorter-growing lilac-rose.

Filipendula (meadowsweet) is another plant which will stand any amount of moisture, providing the shade is not too dense. *F. palmata* 'Rubra' has fluffy heads of bright rosy-red. A lower-growing species, *F. digitata*, has attractive, ferny leaves as well as cerise-pink flowers. Helleborus need damp soil and at least a semi-shaded spot to do themselves justice, but do not do well in a waterlogged garden. There can be few people who are not familiar with *Helleborus niger*, the Christmas rose, with its almost unreal white flowers in late winter. The lenten rose, *H. orientalis*, is similar, but flowers later on taller stems, and comes in a variety of colours from white to deep purple. It seeds freely, so will spread in compatible surroundings; the seedlings will also have flowers of several colours. There are some good named varieties about now, but they tend to be more expensive, although interesting to the collector. *H. lividus corsicus* has leathery leaves with coarsely serrated edges and delicate apple-green flowers in early spring. The rather unfortunately named stinking hellebore, *H. foetidus*, grows about 2 feet (60 cm) tall and has dark green finger-like foliage and green and purple bell-shaped flowers in spring. It also seeds regularly and is often found wild in the more undisturbed parts of the United Kingdom.

The two genera of **hosta** and **hemerocallis** have many similarities. Both are members of the lily family, and both have tough root systems capable of enduring a wide range of conditions, though they are, for the most part, most at home in good, moist soil in light or dappled shade. Hostas produce broad leaves with deep, parallel, longitudinal veins and are mostly grown for the colour of their foliage, which can be green, glaucous-blue, golden, or variegated green and white, gold and white, or glaucous-blue and gold. Some varieties have wavy edges to their leaves. The variegated forms prefer shade which is not too dense, and the golden varieties must have at least some sunshine or they tend to turn pale green. The foliage may be the major attraction, but the flowers, spikes bearing lily-shaped blooms, should not be forgotten as they are pretty in a gentle sort of way. Most forms have violet, lilac or mauve blooms, but some varieties are white, and a few, especially the large, green-leaved, white-flowered 'Royal Standard', are fragrant. Although hostas are recommended frequently as marginal plants, they will stand quite dry conditions and so are very versatile. There are so many good varieties available now it is impossible to list all the excellent ones around, but to begin with look for *H. sieboldiana* 'Bressingham Blue', which makes a superb large plant with enormous blue-sheened, blue-green leaves and tall white flowers, 'Gold Standard', a medium-sized variety from America with bright gold leaves edged with dark green and, where space is limited, try *H. undulata* 'Medio-variegata', which has smallish cream-variegated leaves with wavy edges.

Hemerocallis are better known as day lilies, because of their habit of producing lily-shaped flowers on stems about 3 feet (1 metre) long which only last a day, though the spike itself flowers for many weeks throughout the summer as each new bud on it opens. The plants have long, strap-like leaves, and the flowers come in a large selection of colours ranging from pale yellow and orange to red, mahogany and purple. Nurseries specializing in day lilies will be able to offer numerous varieties and anyone wishing to grow hostas and hemerocallis in a big way would be well advised to join the British Hosta and Hemerocallis Society (Hon. Membership Secretary, Mrs D Stevens, 42 Fairoak Drive, Eltham, London SE9 2HQ).

Peltiphyllum peltatum is an unusual plant with leaves shaped like parasols and with crinkled edges. The leaves are about 3 feet (1 metre) tall and appear after unbranched pink flowers in spring. The plant is quite happy in fairly moist soil, although if the position is too dark the flowers tend not to be so good.

Most **primulas** like damp or moist conditions, but many of them will not give a good performance in really heavy shade. *Primula japonica*, *P. alpicola*, *P. pulverulenta*, *P. bulleyana*, *P. burmanica*, *P. chionantha* and *P. sikkimensis* are all tallish candelabra types in various colours and I find that, although their favourite position is partial shade, or even full sun if the ground is consistently moist, they will flower quite well if there is no sun at all, providing the shade is not too heavy (for example, an area surrounded on all sides with buildings would not be suitable).

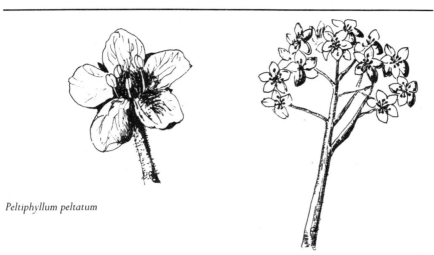

Peltiphyllum peltatum

Ajuga. I have included the versatile 'Bugles' here because, although they like a sunny spot which is not too dry, and even a semi-shaded woodland site, they will grow quite well in shaded, moist positions, and even in water, where they produce long, white water-roots. *Ajuga metallica* (purple leaves, blue flowers), *A. reptans* 'Burgundy Glow' (variegated with wine-red shadings), and *A. reptans* 'Variegata' (cream and green variegated) all make useful carpeting plants which will cover large areas in time and can be used as interesting ground cover between taller plants.

Rodgersia, **rheum** and **gunnera** are grouped together for their major point in common: they all produce large, rhubarb-shaped leaves, so they are not plants to use in the small plot! Rodgersias, in general, provide frothy stems of flowers rather like aruncus and astilbe, but they have a bonus attraction in the statuesque leaves which in many cases are tinted or distinctly coloured purple. Perhaps the most desirable species is *R. pinnata* 'Superba' with a profusion of pink flowers in July and August and elegant bronze leaves.

Rheum, the giant rhubarb, makes a magnificent specimen plant where space allows – but unfortunately it often does not. *Rheum palmatum* 'Rubrum' grows to about 5 feet (1.5 metres) in height, with tall, branching spikes of red flowers in May, preceded by pink, red and purple young leaves turning green as they mature. There are two smaller forms, *R. alexandrae*, which has papery-yellow bracts, and *R. kialense*, with broad, pointed leaves of shiny green and silver-pink flowers.

Gunnera manicata is the monster of the group. The leaves are, frankly, huge and the flowers resemble besoms. Shade and moisture do not trouble gunnera, but frost does, and once the leaves have died down in autumn, the crowns should be protected with a litter of straw, bracken or similar.

It is a misconception that all **ferns** like damp shade, but there are several which do. Included in these are the Maidenhair ferns *Adiantum pedatum, A. pedatum minor,* and the easiest of these, *Adiantum venustum*. Most forms of dryopteris also prefer damp shade, and *Matteuccia struthiopteris*, the ostrich feather fern, likes it quite moist and cool.

There are a few **grasses** which are useful for the sort of situation we are thinking about. *Deschampsia caespitosa* 'Bronze Veil' forms clumps with bronzy sprays of flowers up to about 4½ feet (1.4 metres) high and will even tolerate acid conditions, which many grasses find unacceptable. Many varieties of miscanthus will grow reasonably well if the shade is not too dense and the ground waterlogged. Bamboos, also members of the grass family, will survive in damp, shady positions. The most easy to find are the 13-foot (4-metre) high *Arundinaria murielae*, the quick-spreading *A. nitida* and *A. palmata*, both reaching about 9 feet (3 metres) in height, and the variegated *Pleioblastus viridistriatus (A. viridistriata)*. Bamboos have the tendency to become invasive once they get established, so have to be watched for any potential takeover, but they do have their uses in filling up awkward spots quickly.

Trees and shrubs

Unless their feet are actually dipping into water, most shrubs find it harder to cope with dry shade than damp, sunless places. You will find, therefore, that many of those I list as being suitable for dry shade will do equally well in damp positions, unless it happens to be a bog. The exceptions to this are box, cotoneaster, *Euonymus fortunei* varieties and holly, which do not like getting their roots wet for too long at a time. Otherwise all the shrubs recommended for dry shade are worth a try in damper conditions.

There are also some species which thrive in a waterlogged site. Perhaps the name that springs most readily to mind is **willow** (salix). Most willows get far too big for the average domestic garden, so steer clear of those that rapidly grow into large specimens, like the over-planted weeping willow (*Salix × chrysocoma*), white willow (*S.*

alba, silver willow (*S. sericea*), scarlet willow (*S. 'Chermesina'*), cricket-bat willow (*S. × caerulea*), violet willow (*S. daphnoides*) and the common osier (*S. viminalis*), unless you are prepared to cut them back to ground level readily.

Having said this, I saw a most unusual hedge in Devon this year, which had been created by 'laying' and weaving *Salix caprea*, the pussy or goat willow, and which was actually growing in the water at the side of a large pond. The weeping pussy or Kilmarnock willow, *S. caprea* 'Pendula' is a much more suitable tree for a modern garden, and you could also try the corkscrew willow, *S. matsudana* 'Tortuosa', which is also a more reasonable grower. For the larger garden, the early-to-catkin *S. aegyptica* will provide interest.

There are some much smaller, shrubby species which are well worthy of a place in the garden. *Salix apoda* is a creeping form which produces very large catkins in spring. Another shrub which is covered in catkins is *S. hastata* 'Wehrhahnii' and there are some willows useful for winter stem colour if cut back annually, like the yellow-barked 'Vitellina'. A good variegated shrub is *S. integra* 'Albomaculata' if the shade is not too dense, but to keep it within bounds it should be cut hard back regularly. This has the added advantage of encouraging better variegation. In heavy shade, avoid planting grey, woolly-leaved varieties like *S. lanata* and *S. helvetica*, which do prefer a bit of sun.

Another shrub synonymous with moisture is **cornus**, the dogwood. The young bark is brilliant red, especially on the plain green form; some of the variegated varieties, like *C. alba siberica* 'Elegantissima' and *C. spaethii* tend to have bark of a darker red. In fact, *C. alba* will thrive in all kinds of places providing the soil is not bone-dry, but the variegated types are inclined to lose their colour in full shade. For this situation, *C. sanguinea*, the common dogwood, is more appropriate, although the stems are not so striking. *C. stolonifera* 'Flaviramea' has yellow stems which contrast well when planted with the red-stemmed forms.

Two native species of **viburnum** are very obliging in shady and damp places. *Viburnum opulus*, the guelder rose, and the varieties 'Compactum' (a smaller form) and 'Fructo-Luteo' (which has yellow berries instead of red) make attractive shrubs which colour up well in autumn. *Viburnum lanata*, the wayfaring tree, is covered in heads of white flowers in early summer, followed by red berries turning black, but it is not a tree for a small garden.

Hydrangeas, as one would imagine from the name, are not easy to over-water, and they prefer some shade if their flowers are not to fade quickly. As a change from the usual mop-head and lace-cap forms, you might like to try one of the species like the compact *H. quercifolia*, the oak-leaved hydrangea, with white, pyramidal flower panicles, or *H. preziosa*, also small, with reddish stems and young leaves and salmon-pink flowers. One of the best shrubs to flower late in the season is *Hydrangea villosa*, a much taller plant with long, pointed grey-green leaves and flowers which are blue umbels of lavender florets.

A fast-growing, medium-sized tree for a damp, shady spot is the box elder, **Acer negundo**. This has many variegated cultivars, but I

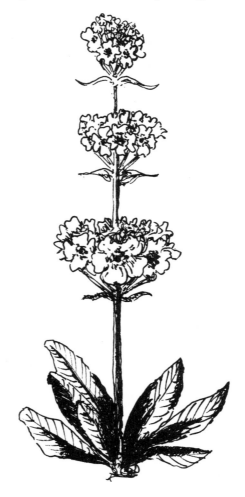

Primula japonica

find that they tend to revert in dark places, eventually losing the variegation completely and becoming all green if the reverted branches are not removed immediately. However, for a moist position in light or half-shade, the cultivar 'Flamingo' is worth planting. This contains pink variegations as well as cream, which are improved by cutting it down every year or every other year, which also keeps it a more manageable shrub.

Sambucus, the true elder, is another species which will take more or less anything that is thrown at it, although I doubt if many people would think of planting the common form, unless they are very fond of wine-making. *Sambucus nigra* 'Aurea', the golden-leaved cultivar, is almost as obliging, but *S. racemosa* 'Plumosa Aurea' is much more choosy, needing a reasonable amount of light in order to keep its colour. There are also forms with cream and golden variegated leaves and ones with purple tints which are worth looking out for.

I would not recommend planting the common **snowberry**, *Symphoricarpos albus*, or the similar *S. albus* 'Laevigatus' unless you have to, because although it will grow in virtually any situation, it is not as easy to remove as it is to establish. There are some better behaved species, though, like *S.* × *doorenbosii* hybrids 'Magic Berry' (short growing with small, carmine berries), 'Mother of Pearl' (semi-pendulous with large berries tinted pink), and 'White Hedge' which has a narrow habit making it suitable for tight spaces.

Rhamnus frangula, the native alder buckthorn, will grow in most shady, damp spots, but prefers a peaty soil or one containing some leaf-mould. Its leaves turn bright yellow in autumn and the red berries which turn black are attractive to birds. The true alders will get too big for most gardens in time, but make good screening trees where the soil is very heavy and wet.

There are two small shrubs which make good ground cover amongst taller plants. **Pachysandra terminalis** and *P. terminalis* 'Variegata' grow less than 1 foot (30 cm) tall and do not seem to mind either wet ground or lack of sunlight. They spread by means of rooting, suckering stems, but are not rampant and do not get out of hand. **Sarcococca hookeriana digyna**, *S. h. humilis* and *S. ruscifolia* are three evergreen shrubs which make up for their insignificant appearance by producing very sweetly scented flowers in late winter. *S. h. digyna* is the largest of these, growing up to 5 feet (1.5 metres) tall. It has narrow, bright green leaves which are not particularly

Sarcococca hookeriana digyna

striking but as it spreads by means of suckers it can be used to fill a place where nothing else will grow. *S. h. humilis* produces dense thickets of stems about 1½ feet (45 cm) high. The bushes spread to cover about 3 feet (1 metre) after a while, and the oldest stems should be cut out after flowering. *S. ruscifolia* will reach about 3 feet (1 metre) eventually, with shiny, oval leaves. It is a slow grower, and useful for that odd dark spot where nothing else seems to survive.

Bergenia 'Sunningdale' – a good plant for light, dry shade

Conifers

There are very few conifers that take kindly to either shade or extremely damp conditions. As a rule I would always recommend that conifers should be given an open position with soil which is not over-dry, but certainly not soggy. However, there are some which would survive the kind of situation we are looking at here, which I feel are worth a mention.

Thuja plicata is often used as a coniferous hedge where the ground is too wet for other conifers, and it will tolerate shade providing it is not too dense. Most dwarf thujas need more exacting growing conditions, but a recently introduced medium-sized cultivar 'Smaragd' will stand some moisture and shade. An attractive tree, it is a pleasant green colour and compact in shape. Perhaps it is a pity to consign it to such a fate as we are describing.

The swamp cypress, *Taxodium distichum*, is a deciduous conifer with a pyramidal form, and will reach about 16–17 feet (5 metres) in ten years in good conditions. It revels in a deep, moist soil, though it does not take kindly to permanent standing water and cold, heavy ground. *T. ascendens nutans* is a smaller tree with a very narrow habit and not as often seen.

Metasequoia glyptostroboides is another strong-growing deciduous conifer which needs a parkland setting to do it justice, but the young plant makes an interesting small tree for a damp, sunless place as it has pretty, feathery foliage and colours well in autumn. It must be removed before it becomes a nuisance if it outgrows its position.

Cedrus deodara, the deodar cedar, grows extremely healthily on the riverbank behind my home, where it is shaded for most of the day with buildings. It occupies a good half of my neighbour's lawn, and although the bottom branches have been removed, very little grows underneath it. The deodar is a beautiful tree, but needs careful siting.

The **silver firs**, *Abies grandis* (grand fir) and *Abies koreana* (Korean fir), will put up with all manner of inhospitable conditions. The grand fir gets much too large for most gardens, but *Abies koreana* only grows to about 6 feet (2 metres) in ten years, so is a good choice for a moist, shady piece of ground, with its fresh green foliage having white undersides to the needles, and long, dark cones, even on young trees.

A successful moist-shade planting

Dry shade

Dry shade generally occurs directly under the canopy of a large, dense tree or against the north side of a wall, where rain seldom reaches and all sun is excluded. The worst sort of dry shade is found under coniferous evergreens. Not only do sun and rain fail to penetrate, but the resinous foliage as it dies and drops to the ground forms a virtually waterproof and slightly toxic mulch.

Dry shade is more difficult to deal with than moist shade, because both elements necessary for the survival of most plants – sunlight and water – are missing. There are very few plants indeed which will grow well enough to look decorative without any moisture at all and so if you really want a good display in this kind of situation you must be prepared to give a certain amount of maintenance.

Preparation of the soil is particularly important. The incorporation of water-retaining material is essential. This can be in the form of well-made garden compost, farmyard or horse manure, composted bark, peat, spent mushroom compost and the like, but it should be added in sufficient quantities to be effective. The soil in dry shade is often dusty and of poor texture and digging in humus-forming material can make all the difference between being able to grow good-looking plants and being stuck with miserable specimens.

It may be necessary to resort to artificial watering during dry periods, especially in summer, and particularly when the plants are young. If enough organic material has been added, a good soaking once a fortnight, or less, may be enough, but if peat has been used as the soil conditioning material it should never be allowed to dry out completely as it can be virtually impossible to wet it again.

I hate to be defeated in the garden and I usually find there is something tailor-made to fit any situation if you are aware of it, but I have to admit that the dry shade under mature conifers is one instance where it may be better to abandon all thoughts of planting, as anything trying to survive in that position seldom, if ever, looks happy enough to make a useful contribution to the garden. It is so dark and the soil so dehydrated that plants have a real struggle to establish themselves.

There are only two species I have seen growing with a reasonable amount of alacrity in this sort of position. One is the rampant variegated dead-nettle, *Lamium galeobdolon* 'Variegata', which spreads rapidly just about anywhere and becomes a real pest in less daunting areas, although with its silver-speckled leaves and yellow flowers it is quite appealing. Please don't let my comments about this one particular variety put you off the lamium family in general, as there are other members which are very handy for dry, shady spots providing they are not too dark. *Lamium maculatum* has pink flowers and marbled leaves, while *L. maculatum* 'Aureum' has golden foliage. 'Beacon Silver' is silver-white, and 'White Nancy' has white flowers and grey leaves.

The other species you might like to try if you are desperate to grow something under a conifer is *Viola labradorica* this is a really pretty little plant, but do think twice about introducing it into your garden as it seeds so readily that it can take over large areas in time. It has purple leaves and violet-like blue flowers, and produces huge amounts of seed. The seedlings soon start to spring up everywhere – in the middle of clumps of alpines, between the cracks of a path, in tubs and containers – in my garden it has even established itself around the top of the drain taking water from the kitchen sink. It rapidly produces a tough, woody root system which is difficult to pull out as it usually just breaks off, new tops appearing even healthier than before.

The problem with planting anything under conifers is that there is a lot of debris falling throughout the year from the older branches. This can bury even *Viola labradorica* after a while, but if you attempt to clear it up too often the plants themselves become damaged. It is sad, but often the best effect is obtained if the ground beneath thick evergreens, and especially conifers, is left totally bare and periodically just tidied up.

We mentioned on page 20 that paving was unsuitable in damp shady places because of the algae which soon make it treacherous. This is not the case where the shade is in a dry position. Dry spots tend to be less humid and it is more difficult for algae to invade the surface, though some lichens sometimes like to have a go. In some gardens it may really be more sensible to forget about growing something in dry shade and opt for attractive paving or gravel instead. Generally, sweeping is a more acceptable chore than watering, and well-laid slabs or concrete can sometimes look better than half-enthusiastic plants.

My comments about making sure that plants for damp shade really thrive under those conditions apply equally to dry shade. Plants relying on plenty of water to grow well will soon shrivel if they do not receive enough, and whereas there are many species which, although enjoying dry shade, survive equally well in damper soil, there are fewer which prefer a moist environment but will grow satisfactorily in a drier position. Hostas are one example; provided the soil is not dust-dry they seem quite able to give a good display in dry shade. Hellebores are another group which will cope with some dryness if they are not exposed to full, hot sun. The day lilies, hemerocallis, manage to grow immediately under deciduous trees,

Helleborus niger

but tend not to flower quite so well. I have several ajugas in quite a dry spot under an apple tree, and they survive quite well, except they seem prone to mildew if they get less water.

It is interesting to note that while there are quite a number of herbaceous plants revelling in moisture but tolerant of drier soil, there seem to be fewer shrubs. Snowberry is perhaps the most obliging; plant it anywhere and it is a difficult thing to snub. Again, I manage to grow *Pachysandra terminalis* and *P. terminalis* 'Variegata' equally well in both damp and dry places. Sarcococca will also grow in a wide range of conditions. Usually, though, as I said earlier, it is shrubs tolerant of dry shade which will also tolerate damp shade, rather than the other way round.

We have already discussed on page 21 why it is difficult for annual plants to establish themselves in shade; dry shade is just as much of a problem to them as damper soil. I cannot think of any hardy annual which could be recommended for dry shade, and whereas there are one or two bedding plants which one can get away with if the soil is damp, there is only one I could suggest for an area which is short of moisture, and that is our old friend, the useful fibrous-rooted begonia, which seems capable of giving a good display regardless of where it is planted.

From my foregoing comments, it would appear that if you have a dry, shady area in your garden and you wish to grow something in it, your cause is lost before you begin, but this is not in fact true, as there are quite a number of easily obtainable herbaceous plants, shrubs and conifers which, properly looked after, give a very adequate show. There is even one bulbous plant, the hardy cyclamen, which will flower well if the shade is not too dense. The most widely grown **Cyclamen herderifolium** (formerly *C. neapolitanum*) has rose-red or white flowers in late summer and autumn and seeds freely into quite poor soil. An early flowering species, *C. coum*, flowers in February and March. There are many others obtainable in the UK, usually from specialist nurseries.

Hardy herbaceous perennials for dry shade

Otherwise known as elephant's ears, **bergenia** is a tough, attractive perennial with large, thick leaves, a woody, rhizome-like root system, and pink, red or white flowers in spring. Several varieties, like 'Abendglut' ('Evening Glow'), *Bergenia cordifolia purpurea* and 'Sunningdale', have foliage which changes to purple or reddish-brown in winter, giving a very good effect. The best white is probably 'Bressingham White'. 'Admiral' has particularly good, glossy foliage

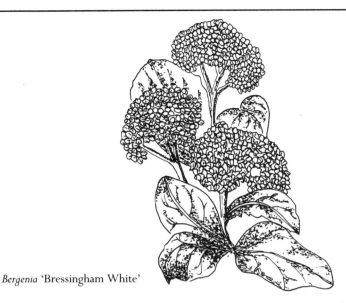

Bergenia 'Bressingham White'

which sets off the red flowers perfectly.

Brunnera macrophylla, the perennial forget-me-not, is a strong-growing, short perennial with large, broad leaves and sprays of blue flowers very similar to the true forget-me-not. It has a more exacting variegated form, which is beautiful, but more difficult to establish, and it does not like full shade. 'Langtrees' is another variegated form with spotted leaves which tolerates darker situations.

Epimediums do not like dust-bowl conditions, otherwise they are very unexacting. They flower in spring and have leathery, low-growing foliage. Many varieties are now available; *Epimedium perralderianum*, with yellow flowers and almost evergreen leaves, is perhaps the most widely sold. *E. cantabrigensis* is a vigorous grower with browny-orange flowers, *E. × rubrum* has red, star-like flowers and *E. × youngianum* 'Niveum' has white flowers.

Euphorbia is a large family of plants, many of them extremely beautiful and exotic, although in fact quite easy to grow. There are several species which must have full sun, but others cope well with dry shade. They mostly flower in late spring and early summer. *E. robbiae* is another of those plants you may wish you had never planted, as it spreads and seeds all over the place. It has dark green, evergreen leaves about 2 feet (60 cm) tall and heads of sulphur-yellow flowers. A species which is becoming more widely known is *E. amygdaloides* 'Rubra', which again does not want too dry a position, but in the right spot makes a delightful clump of red stems and leaves darkening with age, which are a good contrast to the greenish-yellow flower heads. *E. polychroma* also grows about 2 feet (60 cm) tall and has sulphur-yellow flower heads.

Houttuynia cordata **Plena** is a moisture-loving plant, but its variegated relative 'Chamaeleon', with leaves of red, yellow, green and bronze, is a striking variety which seems to tolerate quite dry conditions if the shade is fairly light.

Solomon's seal (*Polygonatum multiflorum*) is a well-known, invaluable plant for conditions of dry shade. It looks rather like a giant lily-of-the-valley and will establish itself virtually anywhere.

Solomon's seal

There is an equally trouble-free variegated form in *P. multiflorum* 'Variegatum'. A similar variegated variety *P. odoratum* 'Variegatum' requires slightly less dry conditions.

Pulmonaria (lungwort or spotted dog) do not object to shade at all, but if the site becomes very dry they tend to sulk, wilting badly, though a thorough watering brings them up smiling again within minutes. Pulmonaria flowers are small, delicate and early, in shades of pink, blue and white, but the most interesting thing about them is their leaves, which are comparatively large, covered in coarse hairs, and often variegated or spotted. Perhaps my favourite is *P. saccharata* 'Argentea'. This is not variegated, but has leaves of an overall silvery-white, with a bonus of pink-budded blue flowers. *P. rubra* 'Redstart' is a non-variegated form, but what makes it special is the fact that its rosy-red flowers last for several months from early spring. *P. saccharata* 'Bowles Red' is a strong-growing plant and useful for space-filling, as is its blue counterpart 'Highdown'. 'Sissinghurst White' is possibly the best of the white-flowered varieties, and 'Marjory Fish', perhaps the most typical of the family, with mottled silver and green foliage and both blue and pink flowers. This form will tolerate quite dry conditions, so makes useful ground cover under trees.

Although **violets** prefer a woodland environment, most of them will thrive and seed well in ordinary dry shade. *Viola odorata* is the old-fashioned sweet violet of cottage gardens, but there are white, apricot and yellow forms available also, although these are not scented. Violets can become quite invasive, so unwanted seedlings should be removed as soon as spotted.

Common violet

Waldsteinia ternata is an evergreen carpeting plant with shiny leaves similar to that of a strawberry and potentilla-like yellow flowers in spring. It is an easily grown, adaptable plant which does equally well in sun or shade and makes useful ground cover.

Shrubs

Box is fairly well-known as a hedging plant, but it has other uses. It makes a first-class container shrub, as it can be clipped and otherwise trained into all manner of different forms: pyramids, balls, spirals and other topiary shapes. The dwarf box, *Buxus sempervirens* 'Suffruticosa', makes a good dwarf edging plant in shade. The best silver box is *B. sempervirens* 'Elegantissima', which makes a good specimen shrub or slow-growing hedge, but there are many other species available if you look around.

The **cotoneaster** family is perhaps best known for the rather over-planted but still attractive fishbone cotoneaster, *C. horizontalis*, which has the useful attribute of being able to cover a wall in any position without needing support. There are many other species and varieties, however, all of which thrive in sun or shade, damp or dry soil. Many are totally prostrate, like *C. humifusus* (dammeri) and 'Skogholm Coral Beauty', while those like *C. conspicuus, C. thymifolius* and *C. microphyllus* form evergreen humps. Several species, for example *C. bullatus*, 'Cornubia', *C. divicarus, C. franchetii, C. frigidus, C. lacteus, C. rotundifolius, C. salicifolius floccosus* and *C. simonsii* are excellent evergreen or semi-evergreen tall shrubs which, trained up on a single stem, make good small trees for modern gardens. All cotoneasters have white or pinkish flowers in early summer, followed by masses of red berries. They are good wildlife garden plants as the flowers are very popular with bees and the berries bring birds flocking in.

A close relative is the **hawthorn**, crataegus. The native may, *C. monogyna*, makes both a good barrier for dry shade and a useful tree. There is a narrow form 'Stricta', but for smaller gardens the species *C. oxycantha* and its pink, red and double-flowered forms are more suitable as they are less strong-growing. *C.* × *grignonensis, C.* × *lavallei*, and *C.* × *prunifolia* are species with large flowers and berries and very bright autumn colour.

Aucuba (spotted laurel). *Aucuba japonica* has been widely planted in public places in the past as it is virtually indestructible. It has large, glossy leaves which are similar to the true laurel but tend to have a serration around the edges. The female plants bear large red berries if pollinated by a male. *A. japonica* will stand really dense shade; if there is more light there are some very nice variegated forms such as 'Crotonifolia', with large gold-speckled leaves, 'Picturata', which has a bright golden centre to the leaves, 'Variegata' (another speckled-leaved variety), and 'Salicifolia', a green, narrow-leaved form which is a good berrying variety. *A. japonica* stands pruning well and so can be kept quite small, or used as a hedge for a shady place.

The most popular **elaeagnus**, *E. pungens* 'Aureo-maculata' is seen in nearly every garden now. It is a leathery-leaved evergreen which can grow quite tall in time, and is green with a bright gold splash in the centre of the leaves, which have a greyish indumentum on the back. *E. pungens* 'Aureo-maculata', and a similar form, 'Variegata', prefer some sunlight, though they do not lose their colour as easily as some variegated plants in full shade. For a totally trouble-free elaeagnus, choose *E. ebbingei*, a greyish-green, spiny, fast-growing shrub which withstands salt-laden gales and the overhang of trees with the same nonchalance. It is possible to obtain two coloured forms quite easily: *E. ebbingei* 'Limelight', a subtly variegated, quick-growing shrub, and 'Gilt Edge', which is much slower but gets fairly large after some years.

Euonymus is another large family, mostly shade-tolerant. The deciduous spindleberries are often found growing wild; they have curiously shaped seeds and most of them colour up magnificently in autumn, although this coloration is better in partial sunshine. *E. alatus* has unusual 'winged' branches, while *E. europaeus* and its variety 'Red Cascade' berry well. *E. yedoensis* has pink fruits as brilliant autumn colour in the right situation.

The evergreen forms of euonymus will cope well with very dry soil. There are dozens of good variegated cultivars, like *E. fortunei* 'Emerald Gaiety', 'Emerald 'n Gold', 'Golden Prince', 'Silver Pillar', 'Silver Queen', 'Sheridan Gold' and 'Sunspot', and for really dark positions there are the all-green 'Colorata', 'Dart's Blanket', 'Emerald Cushion' and 'Vegatus'. Many evergreen euonymus will climb slowly up walls and trees as well as spreading across the ground, so have a dual role to play.

The evergreen spindle tree, **Euonymus ovatus**, and its variegated forms make good taller shrubs for a shaded position, but they can be damaged by frost in really bad winters, although they are known to be very tolerant of salt.

It would be impossible to list all the good **ivies** around these days – every year more and more forms come onto the market. Ivies (hedera) are one of the few species which will retain variegated colour regardless of how dark a situation is. The large-leaved forms, *H. canariensis* and *H. colchica*, are extremely striking, especially the variegated cultivars *H. canariensis* 'Variegata', and *H. colchica* 'Dentata Aurea' and 'Paddy's Pride'. *H. helix*, the common ivy, has many attractive cultivars, both variegated and plain green: 'Cristata' has crinkled leaf edges, 'Chicago' has dark green leaves stained purple, 'Glacier' has silvery-grey foliage, margined white, and 'Gold Heart' is a very popular form, with bright yellow leaf centres. 'Sagittaefolia' has a long, pointed central leaf lobe. 'Marmorata' is mottled silver and grey, with a pink tinge in winter. Ivies are equally useful in shady places as a wall covering or ground cover, and, contrary to the popular misconception, planting an ivy up a healthy tree will not kill it.

Holly, like ivy, is one plant no garden should be without, if only for bringing into the house at Christmas. Again, the variegated varieties are not much affected by shade, and so a well-shaped specimen makes an ideal bush for a shaded corner. There are many to choose from, including the new so-called 'blue' hollies like 'Blue Angel' and 'Blue Princess', which are, in fact, dark greenish-purple, turning more blue in winter. Most hollies are either male or female, so if you want berries you need to plant one of each unless there are a lot of hollies in the gardens surrounding you. One of the nicest, because it is very brightly coloured and almost spineless, is *Ilex* × *altaclarensis* 'Golden King'; despite its name, this is a female. Two other spineless varieties are 'J. C. van Tol' and 'Golden van Tol', which have a well-shaped, pyramidal habit.

There are many good cultivars of the common hollies, *Ilex aquifolium*. I particularly like 'Madame Briot' for its purple young stems and red leaves, turning speckled lime-yellow. The hedgehog holly, *Ilex* 'Ferox', and its variegated forms are curious in that the whole of the leaves, not just the spines, are covered in prickles. One of the quickest variegated hollies to establish is the cream 'Argentea Marginata' which berries well from an early age. If there is only room for one holly in the garden and you particularly want berries, opt for the well-shaped 'Pyramidalis', which is self-fertile.

The **privets** have, in my opinion, an undeservedly bad name. The common privet, *Ligustrum vulgare*, is, admittedly, a rather dreary shrub with sickly-smelling flowers, but the oval-leaf privet, *L. ovalifolium*, is still a good hedging plant for a difficult situation, and its golden and silver variegated varieties, 'Aureum' and 'Argenteum' make very pleasing specimen subjects, especially where there is a flower arranger around, as they will stand any amount of hacking about. *L. lucidum* is a form of glossy leaves and large flower panicles, and has some excellent cultivars like 'Aureo-variegatum', 'Golden Wax', 'Tricolor' and 'Excelsum Superbum'. Although privet is usually evergreen, it can be wholly or partially defoliated in severe winters, but will soon be covered with new leaves again when the weather warms up.

I would not wish that fast-growing, box-like evergreen hedging plant, *Lonicera nitida*, on my worst enemy; it has little to recommend it, growing fast and straggly with a propensity to root from the smallest cutting, making clearing up after clipping a meticulous and arduous task. For a really difficult dry spot, however, **L. pileata** makes a good covering shrub, with a low, spreading, evergreen habit and purple berries in autumn which birds find very palatable.

The **mahonias** are closely related to berberis, but are capable of withstanding much more shaded conditions and they don't have the same treacherous spines. The most obliging is the Oregon grape, *Mahonia aquifolium*, which has evergreen, pinnate, leathery leaves and panicles of yellow spring flowers, with a reddish tint to the foliage in winter. *M. bealii* and the more commonly available *M. japonica*, *M.* ×

Mahonia aquifolium

'Charity' and *M. lomariifolia* grow taller and more upright, and the winter flowers, resembling yellow lilies-of-the-valley, are sweetly scented. *M. pinnata* is another small shrub with quite spiny leaves; a taller cultivar is 'Undulata', thought to be a hybrid between *M. aquifolium* and *M. pinnata*, with dark green, wavy foliage, and a great number of yellow spring flowers.

The **common laurel** (*Prunus laurocerasus*) is a wonderful hedging and screening plant for many shady situations, but it also has some low-growing cultivars which are suitable for planting under trees.

Prunus 'Otto Luyken'

'Otto Luyken', 'Schipkaensis' and 'Zabeliana' are all similar in habit, with shiny, dark green, evergreen leaves and racemes of white flowers in spring, followed by small, cherry-like fruits in autumn which ripen red and later turn black. The visual resemblance to the cherry is the only similarity the fruit of the laurel bears to its edible, deciduous relative, as the berries of the laurel are in fact poisonous.

The **Portugal laurel** (*P. lusitanica*) has smaller, slightly waved leaves, and scented white tassels of flower in May and June. It is hardier than the common laurel, which is likely to be damaged by frost, and it has a particularly good variegated form which will thrive in light, dry shade.

Ornamental brambles are indispensable as fast-growing shrubs in difficult positions. *Rubus tricolor* is a totally prostrate plant which rambles all over the soil, rooting where it touches, so must be used with care. Fully evergreen and producing white flowers in summer, it can also be trained upwards through trellis to thrive where all else fails. A less rampant variety, *R. calycinioides*, forms a close, dense mat with scarlet fruits in autumn. *R. cockburnianus* is a much taller shrub, with white stems and small, purple flowers in June, while *R. tridel* 'Benenden' is a delightful quick shrub for good effect where the shade

Rubus tridel 'Benenden'

is not too dense. It is tall and spreading, with large, white, single scented flowers in May. *R. ulmifolius* 'Bellidiflorus' is a good subject for a shaded, wild corner as it tends to romp away. It has rose-pink double flowers throughout summer. To keep it in bounds, prune it like a blackberry – that is, cut all the old, flowered stems right out in the autumn, leaving the new shoots, which can be tied to a trellis or similar framework if desired.

Ruscus aculeatus is a curious small shrub which produces

clumps of stiff, green stems and dark, evergreen, spiny, leaf-like cladodes with red berries in their centres from September. It will grow in areas of shade where almost anything else would sicken, and is a native European plant.

There are several species of **osmanthus** which do all right in partial shade, but one, *Osmanthus decorus*, is worth trying in conditions of total shade and very dry soil. Otherwise known as *Phillyrea decora*, it has evergreen, dark, willow-shaped leaves which are shiny on the upper surface. The shrub produces small scented white flowers in May, then purplish black berries.

Skimmia, a small, bushy shrub, has become very popular of recent years. There is only one hermaphrodite form, *S. reevesiana*, which will set a crop of berries on its own pollen, but it is not a particularly easy plant to grow, as it must have a cool, leaf mould-enriched root run. The species usually offered for sale at garden centres, *S.* × 'Foremanii' and *S. rubella*, are much easier to grow in dry shade, though they do not like very alkaline soil. To ensure berries, one male should be planted to every two or three females. *S.* × 'Foremanii' is female and has slightly fragrant flowers in early spring; if it is pollinated by *S. rubella* or the less common *S. laureola* it should bear plenty of red berries in late summer and autumn. If there is only room for one skimmia, I would recommend planting *S. rubella* for the attraction of its late winter pink flower heads which are extremely heavily scented. The leaves of all skimmias are aromatic when crushed, those of *S. laureola* being particularly pungent.

The **periwinkles** are invaluable for their quick coverage in any situation. They have long, trailing stems and small or large oval leaves, depending on variety, which in several cultivars are attractively variegated. *Vinca major*, the common greater periwinkle, has dark green shiny leaves and blue flowers in spring. 'Variegata' is similar, but variegated with cream. 'Maculata' is a more uncommon form with lime-green and gold central splashes to the leaves. The lesser periwinkles, *Vinca minor*, are smaller in form. There are many cultivars, such as 'Atropurpurea', which has purple flowers, 'Multiplex' with double purple flowers, 'Bowles Variety', a more compact form with light blue flowers, 'Aureovariegata' and 'Variegata' (gold and silver variegated leaves respectively), and 'Alba', which has white flowers.

Conifers

Although most conifers do not like to be swamped, there are few which will tolerate really dry conditions, especially if there is no sun. One exception is juniperus, the **juniper**, which can stand quite a lot of drought. The golden and grey-leaved sorts need some sunshine in order to retain their colour, but those with green foliage usually take quite well to dry, shady areas. Especially adaptable are the prostrate and semi-prostrate forms like *Juniperus* × *media* 'Mint Julep' and 'Pfitzeriana' (which is unsuitable for all but the largest gardens as it spreads a long way in a short time), *J. communis* 'Green Carpet' and 'Repanda', *J. horizontalis* 'Prince of Wales', *J. sabina tamariskifolia*, and *J. taxifolia lutchuensis*. I do, feel, however, that if you have a problem with dry shade, conifers should only be used as a last resort − most of the other plants described here as being suitable will establish themselves so much more quickly.

Hot, arid places

The really bakingly hot and dry spot can present a terrible problem in a garden. Many of our most popular herbaceous plants and shrubs have their origins in temperate climates, where it is unusual for very high temperatures and rainless periods to be sustained for more than a few days. During the drought of 1976 many normally uncomplicated plants were unable to tolerate the severe water loss they experienced both through abnormal transpiration (moisture loss from pores in the leaves) and their inability to replace it from soil water, and fatalities were extremely high. It took some large specimens several years to succumb totally, and we were still seeing the results of the summer of 1976 into the following decade.

Plants capable of surviving much hotter, drier conditions than they are likely to encounter in the United Kingdom are cunningly modified in one way or another so they can manage with the minimum of natural water. Most woolly-textured, grey-leaved plants originate in either the Antipodes or the Mediterranean area; the grey colouring is usually due not to pigment but to the covering of very fine hairs which give each leaf its own microclimate and stop excess water loss from transpiration. This is why one has to be careful when planting such subjects in many parts of Britain; in cool, shady places where natural rainfall is high the plants become so waterlogged, particularly in winter, that they rot off, or the excessive water both inside and outside the plant becomes frozen during very cold spells, causing fatal frost damage.

Another way plants under drought stress are adapted is by certain parts becoming capable of storing large amounts of water. The most well-known group is, of course, cacti, where the stems have turned into swollen moisture-holding organs, and the leaves are merely spines, soft or prickly, which themselves prevent moisture loss through the rest of the plant. So efficiently adapted are they that they can last for months – even years in some cases – without natural rainfall, using sparingly of their built-in supply instead. In Britain, cacti will not survive outside in most places in winter as the water in them freezes, bursting the cells of the plant, but so long as the temperature does not fall below freezing, they will tolerate quite low temperatures, especially if all artificial watering is withheld.

Succulents form another category of plants which depends for survival on a similar principle to that of cacti. These also store a lot of water, this time in swollen leaves. Again, most succulents are not hardy in the UK for the same reason, but there are one or two which will survive mild winters on the south and south-west coasts, and there are some, like the mesembryanthemum (Livingstone daisy), which make excellent summer bedding plants. It is interesting to note that many alpine plants, which can also be subject to moisture shortage in certain environments, also rely on water-conserving tricks like hairy or otherwise modified leaves, and so their use in the British alpine garden is somewhat limited, better chances of survival being provided through cultivation in an 'alpine house' or similar environment.

A third method by which plants manage to survive on very little water is by dispensing with normal leaves altogether. This is evident in the case of some brooms, which have few, if any, leaves, these being sparse and insignificant, while all their physical functions are performed through the stems. With gorse, the leaves have turned into spines, which present less surface area to the dry atmosphere and so less moisture is able to evaporate from them. In fact, in general those plants which do well in drought conditions have narrow, fine or rolled leaves in order to cut down transpiration to a bare minimum.

Plants which revel in hot spots may also have special flowers. They are often very bright, as they depend to a large extent in insect pollination, do not last very long individually, but are produced in large numbers over a long period, and may close during dull or wet weather to ensure they work to maximum efficiency when it is fine.

It is obvious, then, that subjects needing a fair amount of rainfall and not too high temperatures will have a struggle where the one is at a minimum and the other is at a maximum. If these are to be grown a great deal of artificial watering must be provided, which is a chore, and if for one reason or another the water supply should suddenly cease, as happened in 1976 when garden watering was banned by the water authorities, then the plants will soon be in all sorts of trouble. They will become stunted, the leaves will shrivel and brown, and any flowers will be small, faded and quickly over without replacement.

On the plus side, however, a hot and arid place in the garden is not all bad, providing the right specimens are chosen, and an area of this kind is most certainly not an excuse to rush out and concrete the lot! Many plants of dubious hardiness, like the large-leaved hebes, helichrysums and phormiums, usually do not over-winter because their growth becomes insufficiently hardened by sun, so when they are subjected to freezing, the green cells are seriously damaged. Planted in a hot, dry situation, however, they become much more woody, with less lush foliage; woody cells are more able to survive frost and, even if the leaves are damaged, the mature tissue is able to produce re-growth.

Hot, arid spots usually occur where there is a south-facing bank receiving day-long sun and with little depth of soil to hold water. Another place you will often encounter such conditions is in that part of the garden which both faces south and is close to the property or to a high wall which will keep much of the rain off the ground if the wind is blowing from any direction other than the south, while reflecting and radiating much of the sun's heat back onto the soil.

To ensure that you give any plants intended to be grown in such an area the best start in life, it is necessary to put as much into the soil as you can in the way of moisture-retaining material. While large quantities of fertilizers are not needed as most drought-loving plants originate in poor soil – in fact, too much feeding can be positively harmful as the plants will grow too lush and sappy, an ideal target for frost damage – organic material is required to retain some water; those plants capable of both surviving dry soil and the British climate will not live long if the ground is totally devoid of water. The best medium for this is pulverized bark, which contains virtually no nutrients when it is applied, but rots down gradually and in so doing removes nitrogen from the soil, again ensuring that the plants grow as hard as possible. Peat is less expensive, but can make the soil acid and many of the subjects we are talking about are not too happy with a low pH. Otherwise perlite or horticultural vermiculite can be applied: this improves the rooting capabilities of most plants. If this is done it will enable you to grow other plants – mainly dwarf shrubs – which might not enjoy dust-dry situations, such as spiraeas and potentillas.

It is as well to bear in mind that some of the species which revel in the type of adversity we are talking about are not long-lived plants anyway, and it is a good idea to keep a supply of cuttings handy –

most of them propagate very well from these – so that they can be replaced regularly. Even if they do not die, a lot of them become straggly and untidy in time, regardless of whether they have been well and regularly pruned: young plants often look best.

Annuals

Annuals hardy in the British climate are not a very good bet for the kind of conditions we are looking at, as they tend to grow short and hard, come into flower quickly and equally quickly finish flowering, so all you are left with is a mass of strawy stems, although they do produce large amounts of well-ripened seed so will come again in more or less the same place.

Half-hardy annuals, however, are a different matter. Natives of much hotter climates than our own, they can withstand lower water levels without getting over before their allotted span, and providing they are helped on their way with some watering following transplanting, they should give you a colourful summer with little subsequent effort.

One of the easiest half-hardy bedding plants for any situation is the **French marigold**. There are so many varieties of these available now it would be difficult to single out individuals for special mention – it all depends on your choice of colour and height as to which you grow. If you raise your own plants from seed it will save you a fortune; they are one of the easiest bedding plants to start off providing you have clean compost, good light and a temperature around 65°F (18°C). If you do not mind waiting for flowers until later in the summer, you can even sow direct into the ground at the end of May in a warm spot and, provided the seedlings are kept well watered, they will soon make good, trouble-free plants.

The **bedding salvia**, *Salvia patens,* is also a good choice for very hot places. It is not quite so easy to grow from seed, although in a greenhouse you should not have any problems if you keep the young plants warm enough. If you like the unusual, try 'Dress Parade Mixed'. In addition to the widely recognized red shades there are also rose, pink, purple and white-flowered plants, but to me, salvias will always be epitomized by the brilliant scarlet 'Blaze of Fire'.

Star of the veldt (*Dimorphotheca* or *osteospermum*) is a pretty, daisy-like flower in pastel shades of orange, brown, gold and beige. It is surprising it is not more often grown as it is easily produced from seed, and in all but the coldest parts of Britain may be sown *in situ*.

Swan River daisy (brachycome) is another flower which deserves to be grown more often. The profusion of blue, mauve, purple and white flowers are produced without trouble all summer on compact little plants.

Actually a half-hardy sub-shrub, ***Felicia amelloides*** (blue marguerite) with its pretty blue flower is becoming popular as a bedding plant, especially for container planting, and there is an attractively variegated form. It can be kept from year to year if over-wintered in a frost-free, light position, and strikes easily as cuttings.

Zonal pelargoniums, customarily known as bedding geraniums, positively revel in heat; in cooler conditions the flower heads have a tendency to go brown and mushy. Here again, you can save yourself a lot of money if you grow your own. If you have good plants, you can take cuttings of approximately 3-inch (8-cm) shoots, preferably without a flower (if there is a flower bud it should be removed). This is trimmed off just below a leaf joint, and the bottom leaves are taken off carefully. The base of the cutting is then inserted into damp sharp sand, perlite, vermiculite or an 'open' compost, and, if not over-watered, should root readily. 'Geranium' cuttings should strike more or less at any time of the year, but those taken in late summer and early autumn will be in flower for next year's bedding season.

'Geraniums' are not, of course, annuals, but the recent availability of good seed has helped them to be another victim of the 'throw-away society': it is possible to raise such good plants from seed that it can be easier to grow new plants each spring and discard them in the autumn. The problem with this method of propagation is that in the normal home light levels are not sufficiently high in January (when the seed must be sown to ensure the plants flower early enough in the summer to give the longest possible display) to produce strong, stocky plants, but this problem has been overcome in recent years by many nurseries offering seedlings and young plants at competitive rates for growing on at home.

There is constant breeding research being done on 'geraniums' in the hope of ultimately producing the perfect plant for raising from seed: there are some excellent varieties available already, both F_1 hybrids and open-pollinated kinds, and some seed companies offer pre-sown starter packs which take the hassle out of raising 'geraniums' from seed.

Livingstone daisies (mesembryanthemums) are delightful, carpeting, daisy-like annuals which are usually available in mixed colours, but an early-flowering, all-yellow form 'Yellow Lunette' was introduced a few years ago. The succulent leaves ensure that the plants are oblivious of drought, but they can be disappointing in dull summers as the flowers only open in sunshine.

Portulaca is a similar succulent which is useful for making a bright display in an arid position. It has bright, reasonably large, single or double flowers in a wide range of vibrant colours and is useful for planting on a rockery or between sun-drenched paving.

Wallflowers are capable of tolerating a whole assortment of conditions. They will flower early if given a warm, sunny border, and therefore are useful for filling-in during winter and spring when other bedding plants have been lifted.

Dwarf perennials

Into this category come many plants listed in catalogues as 'alpines', but provided the environment is suitable, they can fulfil all manner of other functions in the garden. They can be especially effective in double-skinned dwarf walls where it is very hot and dry.

Artemisia schmidtiana 'Nana' is a low, spreading, grey-leaved plant with feathery foliage. It is quite hardy in most parts of Britain and can be cut back hard if it begins to look untidy.

Helianthemum, the sun rose, sometimes otherwise known as rock rose is a quick-growing sub-shrub producing double or single flowers in colours ranging from white, yellow, pink and orange, to deep red. Some, like 'Wisley Pink' and 'Wisley White' have the added advantage of grey foliage.

Helichrysum bellidioides has slightly furry leaves and papery white flowers. It will rot off in many rockeries if the climate is damp, but in a sunny, dry bed it can be expected to produce flowers for weeks.

The **hypericum** family includes many shrubs which are useful for dry borders, but also some dwarf sub-shrubs which can be planted where smaller subjects are required. *Hypericum coris, H. reptans* and *H. polyphyllum* all have disproportionately large flowers and a long season, so are very showy little plants.

Lewisia cotyledon hybrids have fleshy rosettes of leaves, at the centre of which appear brilliant yellow, orange or red flower heads.

Wallflower

They are certainly not plants for damp situations, but will give of their best in the arid conditions we are considering at present.

Encrusted saxifrages will withstand dry sites, but are not too keen on really sweltering ones, so must be positioned with care. They produce white, yellow or pink flowers in early summer out of crusty rosettes of bright green or silvery foliage. Highly recommended are *Saxifraga aizoon* 'Rosea' (pink), and 'Luta' (yellow), and *S. cotyledon* 'Southside Seedling', with pink-spotted white flowers.

Sedum is a very large family of plants with thick or succulent leaves enabling them to survive without water for long periods. Our native *Sedum acre* is a pretty but invasive yellow-flowered plant which will live just about anywhere, and as every bit that breaks off will root again, it can become a positive pest. However, varieties of *S. spathulifolium,* like 'Capablanca' and 'Purpureum' are much more garden-trained, as are cultivars of *S. spurium* such as 'Erdblut' (deep green leaves and carmine red flowers); 'Purple Carpet' (purple-red leaves and pink flowers), and 'Variegatum' (variegated foliage and pale pink flowers).

Houseleeks (sempervivum) are well-known cottage garden flowers, with rosettes in many shades of green and red and pink spikes of flowers. Planting them on the roof was thought at one time to keep lightning away, amongst other mythical attributes the plant was thought to have. There are some very good named cultivars available from specialist nurserymen nowadays, including many of the 'cobwebbed' varieties.

Herbaceous perennials

There are not many herbaceous perennials capable of tolerating drought without showing signs of stress, but of those that are, most rely heavily on modified leaves or a covering of hairs to help them to survive.

Artemisia is a family which embraces many herbaceous and 'alpine' plants, as well as some good aromatic shrubs. *A. canesens* produces a mound of silvery-white foliage; 'Lambrook Silver' is a much stronger-growing, taller plant. 'Powis Castle' grows rapidly, with masses of feathery silver leaves, but can be cut hard down to keep it bushy. 'Silver Queen' and the shorter-habit *A. stelleriana* are also worth looking out for.

Dianthus, the fragrant pinks, are a must for any warm, dry garden where the soil is alkaline. The old-fashioned cottage-garden varieties like 'Mrs Sinkins' (white) and its similar pink form only flower in the early summer, but the newer *D. × allwoodii* cultivars like 'Doris' and 'Ian' will produce a succession of blooms throughout the summer.

Tall and dwarf **bearded irises** have a rhizomatous rootstock which must have its top above soil level and obtain a thorough baking in the sun if they are to flower well. They will therefore enjoy the hot, dry conditions we are thinking about, and although they have a fairly limited flowering season in early summer, I feel no garden should be without a collection if space will allow. There are too many cultivars in a host of single and bi-colours from white to chocolate to list any here – to select the few would not do justice to the many.

Kniphofia (red hot poker) requires a warm position, otherwise it can become frost-damaged in hard winters. As well as the orange forms which are so widely recognized, there are some interesting yellow shades like 'Candlelight', 'Little Maid', and 'Percy's Pride'.

Lychnis coronaira **Atrosangunea** has vibrant red, campion-like flowers above hairy grey rosettes of leaves.

Nepeta (catmint) is an aromatic herb which is very useful for edging a hot bed or border. *N. mussinii* is the most widely known, but there are others, like the rather rampant 'Blue Beauty' and 'Six Hills Giant', which is a stronger-growing version of *N. mussinii.*

The most commonly planted **sisyrinchiums** are dwarf species very handy for filling a rockery, but they can become a nuisance as, once established, they start to spread everywhere. There is a taller species, *Sisyrinchium striatum,* which grows about 2 feet (60 cm) tall and has narrow, strappy, iris-like foliage and yellow flowers over a long period in summer.

Some of the taller species of sedum are eminently suitable for dry sites. They include *S. maximum* 'Vera Jameson', with fleshy purple leaves and arching stems bearing late pink flower-heads in late summer, 'Ruby Glow', another succulent plant with purple-grey foliage, and *S. spectabile,* the ice plant so beloved of butterflies in autumn, and its cultivars 'Brilliant' and 'Autumn Joy'.

Stachys lanata (lamb's ears) is another grey-leaved, woolly plant, which produces rather untidy spikes of pink flowers. A more attractive cultivar, with better flowers and larger leaves, is 'Sheila MacQueen', and there is a neat, non-flowering form called 'Silver Carpet'. A new cultivar, *S. olympica* 'Primrose Heron', starts off in spring with yellow, felted leaves, which gradually turn grey before winter. If you want a really vigorous ground cover for a hot spot, there is the light grey *S. byzantia.* There are also dark green, felted forms, like *S. macrantha.*

Shrubs
In the main, shrubs which thrive on drought do not grow too tall, concentrating their energies into producing short, sturdy bushes. The

possible exception is the butterfly bush, *Buddleia davidii,* which will manage with very little water, but the flowers tend to fade even more quickly than normal.

Artemesia arborescens, a shrubby artemisia, grows to about 3 feet (1 metre) high with masses of silvery, filigree foliage very sought after by flower arrangers. The cottage-garden lad's love, *A. abrotanum,* and wormwood, *A. absinthium,* which is more of a woody perennial, are highly aromatic and are easily propagated from pieces of rooted stem and also by cuttings.

Caryopteris × **clandonensis**, and its relatives *C. incana* 'Kew Blue' and 'Heavenly Blue', are otherwise known as blue spiraea from their resemblance to the smaller growing species of that shrub. They have greyish-green, aromatic leaves in late summer and early autumn and are particularly successful on chalk.

Cineraria maritima is a plant which can be placed in several categories. It is usually planted these days as a grey-leaved bedding plant which, although perennial and reasonably hardy, is usually discarded after flowering. However, if it is given a hot, sheltered position it will remain evergreen and continue to grow, until it makes a sub-shrub about 2 feet (60 cm) tall, with yellow, ragwort like flowers in summer. At this stage it can be quite straggly, so it is advisable to cut it hard back in spring after the risk of frost has passed to ensure a profusion of young growth.

Cistus, the true sun rose, is not entirely hardy all over the United Kingdom, but stands the best chance in a hot position where the sun can ripen the wood. Sizes range from quite tall for *Cistus* × *cyprius* and *C. laurelifolius* which are evergreen with large leaves and beautiful white flowers, to compact bushes like *C. corbariensis* (white flowers), *C.* × *crispus* 'Sunset' (sage-green leaves and cerise flowers), *C.* × *lorettii* (glossy foliage and white flowers with a crimson blotch), and *C.* 'Silver Pink' (grey leaves and pink flowers).

Ceratostigma willmottianum (hardy plumbago) is a low shrub, about 2½ feet (80 cm) tall with plumbago-blue flowers in late summer, followed by red-brown seed heads. In favourable areas, where it is not cut down to ground level by the frost, it should be pruned hard back in spring to improve its shape.

Cortaderia (pampas grass) is a well-known plant with vicious, strap-like leaves and, in the named varieties (though not necessarily in the case of inferior unnamed seedlings), striking plumes in early autumn. Two good tall cultivars are 'Argentea' and the slightly shorter 'Sunningdale Silver'. There is a dwarf form 'Pumila', which only grows just over 3 feet (1 metre), though the plumes are taller, and a good variegated-leaved variety, 'Gold Band'. Contrary to what is generally thought, it is not a good idea to burn the old growth off the top of a healthy pampas grass in spring; it may damage the roots. It is enough to cut back the old foliage and pull out as much of the dry debris as possible, wearing very strong gloves.

The **brooms** are reliable, though not long-lived, shrubs for a warm position, with pea-shaped flowers ranging from white to crimson, and habits from prostrate shrubs to small trees. *Cytisus scoparius,* the common broom, has many cultivars, like 'Andreanus' (yellow and chocolate), 'Golden Sunlight', and 'Lena' (bronze). The low-growing species such as C. × *beanii,* C. × *kewensis* and C. *purpureus incarnatus,* all make good subjects for hanging over a dry wall or covering a hot bank. The most commonly planted of the taller forms, C. *battandieri,* the Moroccan broom, has three-lobed, downy grey leaves and pineapple-scented flowers. It is fairly hardy in most parts of Britain, but in colder areas it can be trained effectively as a wall shrub. C. × *praecox,* the Warminster broom, is an easily grown small bush which flowers regularly and profusely in May. There are some good, newish cultivars, like 'Albus' (white), 'Allgold' (a deeper yellow), and 'Gold Spear'. Brooms should be clipped back after flowering to keep them in shape, but not pruned into the old, hard wood, as often they do not shoot again if cut so far down.

A close relative of cytisus is **genista**, which also flowers with pea-like blossoms in spring and early summer. *Genista hispanica,* the Spanish gorse, is a low, prickly bush, but the other dwarf forms, like G. *lydia,* G. *pilosa* and G. *tinctoria* have wiry stems and sparse, insignificant leaves. There is a tall species, G. *aetnensis,* the Mount Etna broom, which produces rush-like stems up to 10 feet (3 metres) tall and flowers in July and August.

Another rush-like broom is the Spanish broom, **Spartium junceum**. The yellow flowers, produced all summer on bushes which can also reach 10 feet (3 metres) if left unpruned, smell strongly and deliciously of honey.

The true **gorse**, *Ulex europaeus,* and its double-flowered form also have much in common with the brooms. Gorse flowers nearly all the year round – 'when gorse is out of bloom, kissing's out of favour' runs the old saying – and the bushes do particularly well on dry, sandy soil.

Hebes make up an enormous family of shrubs and sub-shrubs, some hardy in all but the most inclement places in Britain. The taller, large-leaved species are the least adaptable to cold weather, *Hebe speciosa* especially so, but it, and its cultivars in a wide selection of colours, and some slightly hardier forms like 'Great Orme' (pink), 'Marjorie' (violet and white) and 'Midsummer Beauty' (lavender-purple) can be toughened up a lot if planted where it is very hot and dry. Many of the dwarf and prostrate species, such as the small-leaved, grey *H. pinguifolia* 'Pagei', *H. pimelioides* 'Quicksilver' and 'Wingletye', are first-rate for covering a warm bank. The 'whipcord' hebes, with their almost coniferous appearance – for example the golden *H. armstrongii* and its smaller counterpart, *H. ochracea* 'James Stirling', and the grey-green *H. cupressoides* are also extremely drought-tolerant. There are some very nice small, bushy hebes, such as *H.* 'Waikiki', with narrow purplish leaves which flower throughout the winter in a warm place and make a pleasant contrast to the golden forms, and that pretty little variegated cultivar, *Hebe elliptica* 'Variegata', a plant which becomes upset at the slightest hint of frost but which should come through the winter in the kind of situation we are talking about.

Helichrysum lanatum is a small, grey plant with lavender-shaped leaves and lemon-yellow flowers in July. It is closely related to the tempting aromatic sub-shrub, the curry plant, *H. serotinum*.

Many of the larger species of **hypericum** are adaptable to all kinds of conditions, but *H. × moserianum* and its variegated form 'Tricolor' can sometimes be damaged in severe winters and so make fitting candidates for the hot, dry spot where they can harden in the sun. These two have very large, saucer-shaped yellow flowers with red anthers; 'Tricolor' is variegated green and gold, with red tints and edges to many of the leaves.

Fremontodendron californica is a large, lax, greenish-grey shrub with big, golden, hollyhock-shaped flowers. It is similar to the Moroccan broom in its tendency to flop about and, like the Moroccan broom, it is sometimes better used as a wall shrub. It is not particularly hardy nor long-lived either, but grows quickly so will cover a hot wall in a season or so. Its cuttings strike easily and it is advisable to keep a stock handy in the event of its sudden departure.

It is interesting to note just how many herb-like plants revel in heat, and **lavender** is no exception. The old English lavender, *Lavendula spica,* is one of the most strongly aromatic, although it can get quite large and untidy in time, especially if it is not clipped over annually after flowering. More compact forms include 'Hidcote' (grey foliage and purple flowers); 'Dwarf Munstead' (dark lavender-blue), and 'Twickel Purple'. There is also a white form, and a pink version of 'Hidcote'. The source of oil of lavender is *L. vera,* the Dutch lavender.

Lavatera olbia **'Rosea'**, the tree mallow, quickly makes a large bush with foliage similar to that of fremontodendron and flowers not dissimilar in shape, but of a mallow-pink. Other comparisons can also be made between the two plants: they are both short-lived and can be finished by a hard frost, but are useful for quick effect and are easily propagated from cuttings.

Phlomis fruticosa (Jerusalem sage) is a woolly, grey-leaved bush loosely resembling the true sage, but the leaves are not so aromatic although they have a slight scent when crushed. The flowers are yellow. Cut the bush fairly hard back each spring to keep it in trim.

Phormium has architectural, sword-like leaves with sharp edges, and in certain seasons may produce white flower spikes. *Phormium tenax* (New Zealand flax) is a large, rather untidy plant, but there are several compact cultivars with variegated leaves, such as 'Dazzler', 'Maori Sunrise', 'Purpureum', and 'Sundowner'. Another species – *P. cookianum* – has some good variegated forms, such as 'Cream Delight'. In recent winters many of these brightly coloured varieties have died, but in most very hot situations they should have hardened enough to resist a certain amount of frost, though as a precaution the crowns can be covered with peat, bark or bracken.

The shrubby forms of **potentilla** are invaluable for their adaptability, and they will flower lavishly in a warm, dry place if the soil has been improved as previously described. There are dozens of good varieties to choose from which are freely available from the majority of garden centres, the decision resting on flower colour and height of bush. A really first-class medium-sized cultivar with brilliant yellow, very large flowers, is 'Goldfinger'. 'Abbotswood' is white with grey foliage, which looks good when planted near a purple-leaved hebe like *Hebe* 'Waikiki'. The so-called pink and red forms like 'Princess', 'Sunset' and 'Red Ace' are not to everyone's liking, and can sometimes fade in very bright sunshine, though they do provide an interesting contrast to the yellow varieties.

Romneya hybrida, the shrubby Californian poppy (not to be confused with *Eschscholzia californica,* the annual Californian poppy), is a very beautiful sub-shrub with grey-green stems and glaucous, poppy-like leaves. During summer it produces large, single white flowers with a sweet scent and bright yellow stamens. It can take some time to establish, but in light soil spreads quite rapidly by suckers after a while. I have even seen shoots come up several feet from the parent plant in the middle of a greenhouse!

The **rosemarys** to my mind are some of the most pleasantly aromatic shrubs available to the gardener. The common rosemary, *Rosmarinus officinalis,* makes a large, unruly bush of dubious hardiness in many parts of the British Isles, but a more compact cultivar, 'Jessop's Upright' is hardier and can be used to make a fine hedge for a dry soil. 'McConnells Blue' is a strong-growing, prostrate variety with plenty of blue flowers in summer.

Ruta (rue) is another herb with aromatic foliage, not particularly pleasant-smelling, but certainly very pungent. Common rue, *Ruta graveolens,* has ferny, glaucous leaves and yellow flowers from June to August. 'Jackman's Blue' is a most striking cultivar with blue foliage which is less finely divided and a compact habit which can be further improved by cutting hard back each spring. 'Variegata' is similar to 'Jackman's Blue', but with cream variegations.

The culinary **sages** are invaluable garden plants if there is a cook in the house, but are sometimes not easy to over-winter unless planted in a warm position. The bushes get untidy if allowed to grow unchecked, but careful pruning after flowering will help them to keep some shape. *Salvia officinalis* is the grey-green common sage; the variety 'Icterina' is variegated with yellow. 'Tricolor' is a rather delicate cultivar with leaves variegated cream and purplish-pink, and 'Purpurescens' is the purple-leaved sage. The variegated forms are still suitable for culinary purposes but the flavour is less strong.

Senecio × **'Sunshine'**, formerly *S. laxifolius* or *S. greyi*, is a widely planted, grey-leaved shrub with yellow flowers. Easily grown, it will make a wide-spreading bush in time, but can be cut back annually or biennially to improve its form. *S. monroi* is a smaller species, with wavy-edged leaves which are dark green above the white-felted beneath.

All the **thymes** prefer sunny, dry soil, and many make excellent ground cover for a low bed or warm bank. In addition to common thyme, there are many decorative species and cultivars, including the very dwarf, yellow 'Anderson's Gold', the lemon-scented *T.* × *citriodorus* 'Aureus' and *T.* × *citriodorus* 'Silver Posie', the grey-leaved, pink-flowered 'Porlock', and dozens of carpeting forms like 'Bressingham', 'Doone Valley', *T. herba-barona*, *T. micans,* and varieties of *T. serpyllum* with variously coloured flowers.

Perovskia **'Blue Spire'** (Russian sage) is yet another grey-leaved, blue flowered shrub with slightly aromatic leaves. It has a very narrow habit and for maximum impact should be planted in groups of at least three plants.

Most **spiraeas** will tolerate some degree of dryness, but there are two yellow forms which give the best leaf coloration in very bright

Yucca filamentosa

sunlight. *Spiraea* × *bumalda* 'Goldflame' has been around for some time. The young foliage and tips of the branches are a bright orange-red, softening to yellow with age. If the red flowers are cut off when they start to fade, new red shoots will appear. For the best leaf colour, the bushes should be cut back to the base in spring. *S.* × *bumalda* 'Goldmound' is a much smaller, more compact shrub useful for confined spaces, but the leaf colour is not as intense and the young shoots are less spectacular, also the pink flowers tend to look a little insipid against the yellow foliage. 'Little Princess' is similar, but with green leaves. *S. japonica* 'Alpina' is a dwarf form of 'Little Princess'.

Yuccas are extremely striking architectural plants with their thick, sharp, sword-like rosettes of leaves. In the fullness of time they begin to produce tall, upright panicles of white, bell-shaped flowers. *Yucca filamentosa* (Adam's needle) is the most available species; it has several fine variegated forms such as 'Bright Edge', 'Golden Sword' and 'Variegata'. *Yucca gloriosa* is also freely obtainable; it is a taller plant with a thick, fleshy stem topped with a cluster of sharp-tipped, long, narrow leaves. The creamy-white flowers are sometimes tinged red on the outside. There is also a variegated form of this species.

Hosta 'Royal Standard' – a scented plant for shade
Symphoricarpos 'Mother of Pearl' will recover well after vandal attack
Moisture-loving plants in partial shade (*overleaf*)
An unusual hedge – *Salix caprea* edging the Mill Pond at Docton Mill, Harland
Point, Devon (by kind permission of Mr and Mrs Pugh) (*overleaf*)

Moist, sunny areas

To me, an area of the garden which is both very sunny and very wet is more of an asset than a problem, but I suppose if my whole plot consisted of a bog I would not be too pleased! If the area in question is very large, it might be possible to drain at least some of it, using a network of land drains discharging into a soakaway, ditch or even a specially dug pond, but to give the opportunity to grow as wide a range of plants as possible, at least one part should be left undrained.

However, it is unlikely that the majority of gardens would be faced with this situation on a large scale, as it would have been virtually impossible to build a property on that kind of land in the first place. What is more probable is that one section of the land is poorly drained, either because of water running onto it from another part, or as a result of underground springs, or because the water table is naturally high and the soil on the heavy side.

In such circumstances, the garden-owner should consider himself or herself lucky, and set about making a feature of the problem. To begin with, forget about trying to grow a good lawn, as it will rapidly become overrun with moss. If the soil is very heavy, with perhaps a layer of clay beneath the top layer, it may be possible to dig a pond which will fill naturally from water draining into it from the surrounding land. This may not be quite the wholesome feature it would be if artificially constructed with a liner, but is quite adequate for planting up with a wide selection of aquatic plants which need to be grown in standing water. The areas bordering this would happily support species needing moist or very wet soil for healthy growth.

Euonymus fortunei 'Emerald Gaiety' (*top left, previous page*) will grow in shade or sun

Pachesandra terminalis 'Variegata' (*top right, previous page*) is ideal for shade

A collection of ajuga (*bottom of previous page*) growing in damp shade

Skimmia 'Foremanii' (*top left*) – a useful shrub for shade

Mahonia 'Charity' (*top right*) in a dry, shady place

Prostrate junipers will survive in some shade

If it is not possible to make a pond out of part of the site, you should still have no trouble at all in creating an effective planting. The only point you have to bear in mind is that plants for this situation, just as those for other types of environment, have their particular preferences, mainly with regard to the amount of water they need or can tolerate. Get this right, and there is no reason why the established feature should not be a delight to behold.

Plants suitable for standing water from 12–24 inches (30–60 cm) deep

The **water lily** (nymphaea) is too well-known to need to describe it in detail. The thing to remember when choosing varieties is to select forms of moderate habit, rather than very vigorous ones which would choke the pool. Most larger water garden specialists have a range of suitable named varieties in reds, yellows, pinks and white. A reliable and universally obtainable species is *Nymphaea × marliacea*, with cultivars 'Albida' (white), 'Carnea' (pink) 'Rosea' (a deeper pink), 'Chromatella' (yellow), and 'Flammea' (wine red, streaked with white).

Water hawthorn (*Aponogeton distachyus*) produces white flowers just above the surface of the water from spring to autumn which are 'may' scented. The leaves are flat and float on the surface similarly to the water lily, but they are longer and more narrow.

Ranunculus aquatilis (water crowfoot) is a pretty native species, with dark green foliage and white flowers.

Orontium aquaticum (golden club). This has spikes of yellow flowers projecting 12 inches (30 cm) above the water surface, and should have a rich, deep soil to root into.

Nymphoides peltata (Villarsia nymphoides – floating heart or bean lily), looks like a miniature water lily, with dark-green water lily-like leaves which are reddish-brown mottled. The small flowers stand an inch or two above the water surface during July and August.

Plants suitable for standing water from 6–12 inches (15–30 cm) deep

There are some miniature forms of **water lilies** which will grow well in quite shallow water, providing the level does not drop too drastically. One such is the white 'Candida'; if you prefer a good wine-red, with outer petals of lilac-pink, look out for *Nymphaea × laydekeri* 'Purpurata'. There is a good yellow, 'Pygmaea Helvola', and there is also a most unusual form, 'Aurora', which opens yellow, changing to orange, finally maturing dark red. These very dwarf forms of water lily are not available from every garden centre with a water gardening department, but are usually to be found at good specialist aquatic nurseries.

Alisma plantago (water plantain) has tall, spiked pink and white flowers from June to August and dark green, plantain-like leaves.

Butomus umbellatus (flowering rush) is a pretty native water plant, with 3-foot (1-metre) high stems topped by pink flower heads.

Calla palustris (bog arum) has discreet white flowers followed by showy pods of scarlet seeds.

Caltha palustris (marsh marigold, kingcup of water blob) will grow in ordinary moist soil but thrives in standing water. It flowers in spring and early summer and sometimes there is another flush in autumn. There is a white form 'Alba' and also a good double, 'Plena'. A taller-growing species, C. *polypetala*, is happier growing in wet soil, rather than being totally submerged.

Mentha aquatica (water mint) is a rampant grower which is inclined to get out of hand, but is useful for covering large areas of a wild garden and smells very pleasant. It will grow in virtually any depth of water or damp soil, spreading, where the bottom is too deep for it to reach, by stems producing water roots along their length.

Ranunculus lingua 'Grandiflora' (great spearwort) is another adaptable aquatic which also tends to 'take over' if planted in the wrong place. It produces abundant yellow, buttercup-like flowers all summer, together with thick, fleshy stems and spear-shaped leaves.

Sagittaria sagittifolia (common arrowhead) produces a large number of arrow-shaped leaves through which appear spikes of three-petalled white flowers throughout the summer. It is yet another strong grower which is really only suitable for larger areas.

Scirpus lacustris is a strong-growing bulrush reaching about 5 feet (1.5 metres). Again, it is possibly more suitable for the lakeside than the shallow margins of a pond.

Plants suitable for standing water from 0–6 inches (0–15 cm) deep

Acorus calamus 'Variegata' is a striped grassy plant with reed-like, aromatic, sword-shaped foliage, variegated green, pink and cream. There is also an all-green form which is not so attractive.

Cotula coronopifolia (golden buttons) is covered throughout summer with small, yellow, button-shaped flowers.

Cyperus longus (sweet galingale), a sedge growing to about 3 feet (1 metre), has feathery chestnut plumes of flowers.

Eriphorum angustifolium (cotton grass) should not have more than 3 inches (7 cm) of water over the top of its roots. It has slender stems terminating in silvery tufts and will tolerate acid conditions.

Glyceria aquatica 'Variegata' (manna grass) is a variegated grass with variegations of green, yellow and white, suffused pink in spring. It grows to a maximum of about 2 feet (60 cm).

Hypericum elodes (marsh hypericum) is a low-growing plant with grey-green leaves and yellow flowers. It is a useful plant for a miniature bog garden, where it looks particularly good in association with **Veronica beccabunga**, the brook lime, a dwarf creeping plant with blue flowers.

The native bog iris, **Iris pseudoacorus**, is well-known, with its tall stems of yellow flowers in early summer. There is a form with variegated yellow leaves, which has the rather annoying habit of turning all-green later in the season, but it is quite spectacular when the new foliage emerges in spring. The exquisite Japanese iris, **Iris kaempferi**, which has cultivars in shades of white, blue, violet-purple and red, is not particularly easy to grow and should be planted in very shallow water and acid soil. *Iris laevigata* and its many cultivars will grow in more alkaline soils and are easier to establish.

Manyanthes trifoliata has bold, glossy, bean-like foliage and white flowers with a pink feathering to the edges.

The **musks** will romp away in both shallow water and ordinarily moist soil. *Mimulus luteus* (monkey musk) and its modern cultivars will give a profusion of flowers throughout the summer. *M. ringens* has dark green leaves and lavender-blue flowers.

Myosotis palustris (water forget-me-not) is a moisture-loving form of this pretty plant, with clusters of bright blue flowers in May and June.

Pontederia cordata (pickerel weed) has lush, dark green foliage and light blue flower spikes about 2 feet (60 cm) tall which resemble miniature delphiniums.

Scirpus zebrinus is a striped green and white rush with quill-like stems reaching about 4 feet (1.2 metres).

Typha latifolia, the great reedmace – often erroneously referred to as 'bulrush' – is much too large a plant for all but the biggest ponds, but *T. angustifolia* and *T. minima* are of much more conservative proportions.

Zantedeschia aethiopica, the arum lily, tends not to be particularly hardy if grown out of doors in Britain, but will survive the winter perfectly well if the crown has a covering of a few inches of water. A similar temperamental plant is *Lobelia cardinalis,* which again needs the protection of a 'litter' of peat, bark or hay if grown in the ordinary border, but will come through even really cold weather unscathed if planted in 2–3 inches (5–7 cm) of water.

Damp and wet soils

Many of the plants which are suitable for damp shade will do equally well in a sunny position if the soil is constantly moist. Among those which give a good show regardless of sun or shade are astilbes and filipendula, hostas (especially the golden-leaved forms which retain their colour much better), peltiphyllum peltatum, ajugas, rodgersias, rheum and gunnera.

Astilbe 'Famal'

There are many other plants which must have a wet root-run and their heads in sunshine in order to give of their best. Two of my favourites which deserve to be planted more are the variegated figwort *Scrophularia aquatica* 'Variegata', and the variegated watercress, *Nasturtium officinale* 'Variegata'. The former is a strong-growing plant, very bushy and reaching about 2 feet (60 cm) in height, with serrated, nettle-like leaves very strikingly variegated green and white. The flower spikes are purplish and rather insignificant – it is the foliage which is the main attraction. Variegated watercress is just as eye-catching, with large cream splashes on the leaves. Again, one could dispense with the flowers, which are yellow, straggly and untidy, like cabbages which have run to seed. Also, like the cabbage, this plant has the drawback of being affected by certain of the same pests and diseases, like cabbage root fly and club root, but to my mind, this snag is not serious enough to put you off planting it in a suitable damp place.

Cautleya robusta is an exotic plant which rather resembles the canna. It needs a rich soil, in which it will grow to 4 feet (1.2 metres), with stiff spikes of yellow flowers.

Iris sibirica, the Siberian iris, is a dainty, yet robust, member of the iris family and in recent years many good new cultivars have been introduced which deserve a place in any moist piece of ground. They are available in a range of colours: white, cream, pink, wine red, blue and purple. The blue 'Flight of Butterflies', white 'Limeheart' and pink 'Sparkling Rose' are especially worth growing.

Lysimachia punctata (yellow loosestrife), will grow in virtually any position, but looks healthier if the soil contains plenty of moisture; if it becomes dried out the leaves shrivel up the stems. *L. nummularia* and *L. nummularia* 'Aurea' (creeping Jenny) are ground-hugging prostrate herbaceous plants with small, yellow flowers along the lengths of their stems. 'Aurea' has golden leaves in full sunshine.

Lysichitum americanus, the skunk cabbage, has flowers like a yellow arum and an exotic appearance, accompanied by an unpleasant smell which deters many people from planting what is otherwise a very pleasing flower.

The **Globe flowers** (trollius) produce cupped flowers similar to a half-open buttercup. The flowers are usually yellow, as in the variety 'May Gold', but 'Fireglobe' is orange, and 'Alabaster' is a very pale primrose. Ranunculus is a similar flower with buttercup-shaped leaves and flowers of various sizes, according to variety. *R. aconitifolius* 'Plenus' is covered with small, white double flowers in early spring; *R. acris* 'Flore-pleno' has large, double yellow blooms. *R. gramineus* has grassy leaves and very bright yellow flowers.

Trees and shrubs for moist, sunny sites

Some of the trees and shrubs tolerant of shady, damp spots are just as happy, or happier, in full sun. Amongst these are the willows, guelder rose, alder, *Acer negundo* and cornus. The variegated forms of cornus colour much better with plenty of sun on them, therefore if you have a wet, sunny spot, consider *Cornus alba sibirica* 'Elegantissima' (cream and green variegated), *C. alba* 'Spaethii' (cream and gold), *C. alba sibirica* 'Variegata', another cream and green form but the markings are different and it is less vigorous; *C. alba* 'Aurea' (golden-yellow leaves), and 'Westonbirt', an all-green form but with stems of the most brilliant red which look best with the winter sun shining through them.

Another genus which should not be discounted on the grounds of its bad reputation, but which does extremely well in wet positions, is populus, the poplar. The most well-known species are timber trees and should not be planted within a million miles of a house – well, perhaps I exaggerate! There are, however, a few highly ornamental species of poplar which will cut back without detriment; in certain cases this can even be of benefit to the leaf colour. *Populus candicans* 'Aurora' will grow into quite a large tree if left unpruned, but the colouring of the heart-shaped leaves – creamy-white and pink with dark green – is so much better if it is hard pruned every other year in February. Being one of the 'balsam poplars', the leaves are balsam-scented when opening in spring. *Populus* × *serotina* 'Aurea', the golden poplar, is a pyramidal, golden tree when young, branching out later. If it is pruned in late winter it improves both the shape and the colour.

If the ground is moist, but not completely waterlogged, you could try planting that most useful of garden trees, *Amelanchier lamarckii,* the snowy mespilus. This makes a large shrub or small tree if left to its own devices, but if pruned back periodically, or even clipped over annually (not a good idea for most shrubs) it will fit all but the smallest area. It has something for every season, pinkish-orange foliage in spring, followed by a profusion of single white flowers, after which appear bright green leaves which assume the most brilliant hues in autumn, followed by black berries. If this description appeals to you, do not be deterred by its inclusion in this particular section, as it will thrive in nearly every situation providing the soil is not too shallow and dry.

Areas of very shallow soil

One of the most successful parts of my garden, though the plants in it are nothing out of the ordinary, should not really have been part of the garden at all; in fact, strictly speaking, it is not even in the garden – it is part of the road outside. I am not suggesting you copy my idea as far as the position is concerned, but it shows what can be done with what appears to be an impossible situation.

At present, my border does not narrow the road, but it does prevent vehicles from driving too close to the cottage, while giving a great deal of pleasure to those who take their Sunday afternoon walk past our home.

How this planting came about was purely by accident. When I originally moved to this property, the area which is now such a successful border was merely the joint between a concrete kerb edging a strip of crazy paving under the front windows and the lane running past our cottage. There was no front garden as such, only gaps in the paving, which now are well-filled with pyracanthas, cotoneasters, vincas and prostrate junipers, making a good backdrop to this 'accidental border'.

There is about an 8-inch (20-cm) drop from the top of the kerb to the road surface, creating a trap for all the dust blowing about and the soil dropping off the farm vehicles and sugar beet lorries passing by. I used to clean up the collection of soil and half-rotted leaves, but soon despaired, so the debris lodging there began to build up into a fair imitation of potting compost, followed very rapidly by a nice collection of weeds. First I tackled these by hand, but I began to lose heart as it was rather like painting the Forth Bridge (once finished it is time to start again), so I then resorted to weedkillers.

I cannot remember at what stage the penny began to drop that if weeds would grow, why not intentionally positioned plants? After all, to quote a trite definition, 'a weed is only a plant in the wrong place'.

It is not the sort of situation you would want for all your choicest subjects, but in everyone's garden are obliging, fast-growing things originally brought in to fill gaps, which are gradually replaced by more special acquisitions; and spreading, easy-rooting plants quickly grow large enough to divide into dozens of the same. I started to introduce these into my non-border, and to my delight, following some initial care and attention like extra watering and a thin top-dressing of Levington Compost, they not only survived but began to grow and spread.

The area only receives sun until late morning in summer, and less in winter, which is fortunate in one respect, in that now the plants are established it is only during prolonged dry spells that regular watering is necessary; if the strip were in full sun it would need constant attention. In another it is less fortunate, as any open bits of 'earth' become very mossy during winter, but when this gets too bad I pick the worst of it off by hand. Annoyingly, this also removes some of the precious growing medium, but it can be replaced with good soil or the contents of used growing bags.

The first plants to be introduced were not those I would normally have in my garden: the invasive *Sedum acre* (yellow or biting stonecrop) and the equally rapid-spreading *Sedum album*. I interspersed these with London pride *(Saxifraga × urbium)*, and a plant you often see it associated with, *Sedum spurium*, which also has pink flowers at about the same time.

At that stage, I stood back and waited. Would the plants grow? Would the council come along and remove them? Would the huge lorries from the international haulage company down the road run over them? Would the Saturday night crowd returning home in the small hours find them a suitable target for their 'high spirits'? As luck would have it, they did grow, and all my other fears were groundless, so I decided to put 'stage two' into operation. This was to introduce more colour as the whole scheme looked rather sombre.

In a mad moment, I once bought a plant of the bright yellow-leaved golden feverfew, *Tanacetum parthenium* 'Aureum'. Since then it has thrown its seeds the length and breadth of the garden, plants appearing in paving cracks, hedge bottoms, tubs, gutters, drains, throughout the vegetable garden and in the top of an upturned bucket, as well as in many more conventional places. There were seedlings to spare everywhere so I selected the half-dozen best and planted these at intervals along the strip, together with some surplus Ajuga 'Burgundy Glow', 'Purpurea' and 'Variegata'. The golds, creams, pinks and purples livened the proceedings up considerably.

Flushed with success, my enthusiasm knew no bounds the next

season, and I added other bright and lively items like the variegated dead nettle *(Lamium galeobdolon* 'Variegata') and a plant which I have never ceased to regret planting elsewhere in the garden, the pretty — but seed-happy — purple-leaved *Viola labradorica* 'Purpurea'. Here it is no trouble at all, as it can seed to its heart's content and intermingle with its fellows without becoming a nuisance.

Since then I have experimented with many other things. The nature of the 'soil' means that seeds germinate readily if the ground is moist enough, and a few initial plants of forget-me-nots (myosotis) have distributed their progeny throughout the border. One year I tried a packet of our native heartsease or wild pansy, *Viola tricolor,* and still have young plants appearing. In fact, all pansies and violas seem to thrive providing they start life as seedlings sown in situ. In addition to *V. tricolor,* I now have the multi-coloured 'Bambini', 'Prince Henry' (purple) and 'Prince John' (yellow) which escaped from a nearby hanging basket. The golden feverfew has seeded itself so prolifically that I am having to weed it out. Other 'escapees' are *Helleborus foetidus* and the native gladdon, *Iris foetidissima,* which have come round to the front from the back of the garden; they may become too big in time, but the depth of the soil should stunt their growth somewhat. I hope so; I would like to retain them, for they have added usefully different leaf forms to the planting.

Providing there is at least half a day's sunshine on the border, many of the commoner rockery plants are suitable for shallow soil of this nature. My initial experimental plants have been joined more recently by the yellow *Alyssum saxatile,* various shades of aubretia, again from a packet of seeds sown directly into the bed, and the similar but white *Arabis caucasica. Campanula carpatica* is quite happy, and provides a useful blue to blend with the pinks of the London pride and *Sedum spurium.* The perennial wallflowers are tough and undemanding; I managed to get hold of the many-coloured, semi-prostrate *Cheiranthus semperflorens* 'Jacob's Jacket'; some cultivars get too tall for this particular situation.

Some of the mat-forming acaenas would also be good for these circumstances, whereas in more important places in the garden they can become too much of a good thing. Another ground-hugging plant I intend to add is the tough-stemmed, grey-leaved *Raoulia australis.* Some of the dwarf, iris-like sysyrinchiums are beginning to appear of their own accord, presumably from the rockery behind the cottage, which is many yards away. I have tried planting the creeping thyme, *Thymus serpyllum,* but it took so much longer to get established in competition with all the other more strongly growing species, that I have had to give it more care than the border justified, although two patches are now beginning to take hold. Towards the end of the strip, where there is more sun, house leeks (sempervivums) are spreading to produce some nice big clumps.

Sempervivum

Very recently I obtained a large plant of the variegated form of *Aegopodium podagraria,* which is perhaps better known in its plain green form as that most dreaded of all weeds, ground elder. The variegated variety is not so invasive, but in contrast highly attractive, with a great deal of pale cream on the leaves, a colour which up till that time had been lacking in the foliage of this planting. I split the plant into several smaller ones which were distributed evenly along the length of the border and, as I write, they are just beginning to produce new leaves in the centres. While I would not recommend this plant for everyone's garden, especially if the soil is light, rich or

81

sandy, as you may get more than you bargained for, there is no doubt it has its uses in certain situations, and this is definitely one of them.

Even bulbs have a place in this horticultural hotch-potch. The area is not one to spend much money on, but after Christmas last year our local garden centre was selling off its surplus spring bulbs at knock-down prices, and I could not resist a large quantity of crocuses. I discovered that the surface of the strip adjacent to the crazy paving (where the 'soil' is deepest) could be folded back slightly, rather like the edge of a carpet – the matted roots prevented it from dropping to pieces. This left an open slit, about 6 inches (15 cm) deep, down which the dry corms could be dropped, then the 'mat' could be put back again, burying them. The result was a mass of flowers, only slightly later than if they had been put in at the correct time, and the promise of more to come in following years.

I mentioned earlier how easy it was to get seeds to germinate in this border, and because of this, each year when I top-dress with potting compost or old growing-bag material, I mix in some dwarf hardy annual seeds, and even a few half-hardy ones which will germinate and flower later in the year. The seeds come up at random, many in the middle of species with duller foliage, adding temporary bright colour to the more conservative perennial hues. At the end of this chapter (page 84) is a list of the annuals I have found most suitable. Many of them will seed themselves and come up the following year if not dead-headed, but I always put a few more in with the top-dressing just to be on the safe side.

While the circumstances surrounding this particular planting are possibly unique, it occurred to me that many people may have a similar problem area in the garden which they thought was impossible to plant up, perhaps by the side of a path where the kerb is set in a wide piece of submerged concrete, round a similarly concrete-set clothes post, or where an old path has been buried, for instance. Nearly all the plants I have mentioned will grow regardless of aspect or locality, but, as stressed previously, a very sunny spot will need to be watered a great deal, and if the area is in full shade, most rockery plants and all hardy annuals should be omitted.

To succeed, there should be a depth of soil or similar growing medium of about 6 inches (15 cm), although the ground can be shallower in parts – my particular border tapers to nothing at the front where it adjoins the road surface. Also in my case the solid base was not all that sound: there were cracks and crannies into which the plant roots could work themselves, giving a stronger hold and a cooler root run in hot weather. If it is possible, a very hard base should have one or two holes knocked into it before planting. These need not go through to the ground underneath; the additional earth that will fall into them will be enough to help the plants to become established.

Very little after-care is needed with the subjects I have suggested above once the planting is working properly. You may need to trim the plants back once or twice in the summer to keep them compact and bushy and it will look tidier if the dead heads are removed – but remember not to do this until the seeds have ripened and fallen if you want the plants to multiply by this method! Some of the more enthusiastic species may need shortening back to give the slower ones a chance; this applies especially to the variegated dead nettle and ajuga, and you might like to remove excess seedlings of plants like *Viola labradorica* 'Purpurea' and golden feverfew if they threaten to take over completely. You will also find the odd weed jumping on the bandwagon and this should be pulled out as soon as spotted, although in time the plantings will be so dense that the few which do appear are hardly noticeable anyway.

Hardy annuals
Although the bedding **alyssums** are usually raised as half-hardy annuals, they will germinate quite well if sown straight into the ground where they are to flower. As well as the most widely planted 'Carpet of Snow' and 'Little Dorrit', there is a good purple, 'Oriental Night', a lilac-pink form ('Rosie O'Day'), and a very dark purple variety ('Royal Carpet').

Many varieties of the easily grown annual *Calendula officinalis* (pot marigold) grow rather tall for the type of situation described in this chapter, but one variety, 'Fiesta Gitana', will reach less than 12 inches (30 cm) if the soil is shallow. The bushy plants produce a mass of double flowers ranging from creamy-yellow to orange throughout the summer. Calendulas, unlike many hardy annuals, should be dead-headed as the seedlings do not come true to type; the common pot marigold which usually appears in following years is a tallish, unattractive plant which is prone to mildew and has unexciting single orange flowers.

Candytuft 'Dwarf Fairy Mixed' is, as its name suggests, a dwarf form of candytuft, with flower heads in many shades: violet, purple, crimson, pink and white.

Cornflower 'Baby Blue' is a new, dwarf variety growing less than 12 inches (30 cm) tall, with deep blue flowers 1½ inches (4 cm) across. It may need watching for mildew, which can be controlled with Benlate.

Cotula barbata grows about 6 inches (15 cm) tall and is covered with heads of button-like yellow flowers.

Dahlberg Daisy (thymophylla), an uncommon annual with pretty, single yellow blooms and finely cut foliage, reaches about 8 inches (20 cm) in height.

'Glistening White', a variety of *Dimorphotheca aurantiaca* (see page 54) is a dwarf and compact form of Star of the veldt, growing to 6–9 inches (15–23 cm) in height, but all other forms are suitable.

Echium hycopsis **'Dwarf hybrids'** grow to 12 inches (30 cm) tall. They are bushy plants with flowers in blue, white, lavender and rose.

Eschscholzia californica (Californian poppy) has beautiful poppy-like flowers and feathery, grey-green foliage. The best mixtures, like 'Ballerina' and 'Harlequin Hybrids', include many subtle shades of red, pink, orange, yellow, cream and white.

Scarlet flax (*Linum grandiflorum* 'Rubrum'), will reach about 16 inches (40 cm) in height on good soils. Where the soil is poor, dry or shallow, however, it will make a much smaller plant, while still producing plenty of bright flowers.

Godetia 'Dwarf Bedding Mixed' has azalea-like flowers in shades of pink, salmon, crimson and carmine, with some petals patterned or striped, and many with picotee edges.

Ionopsidium acaule (violet cress) is a very dwarf plant, suitable for cracks and extremely shallow soil.

Larkspur 'Dwarf Hyacinth-flowered Double Mixed' a compact variety of the well-known, delphinium-like annual, with flowers in a wide range of pinks and blues.

Leptosiphon is a tiny, dainty plant with many-coloured flowers, suitable for very shallow soil.

Limnanthes douglasii (poached egg flower) has saucer-shaped flowers in white with a yellow centre. It seeds freely so is ideal for the sort of spots we are looking at.

Linaria toadflax *maroccana* **'Fairy Bouquet Mixed'**, has snapdragon-like flowers in a wide variety of colours. The plants grow about 8 inches (20 cm) high.

Love-in-a-Mist (*Nigella damascena*) is another annual which will grow rather tall in ordinary soil, but it will reach much less than its estimated 20 inches (50 cm) where the soil is shallow and dry. 'Miss Jekyll' is a deep sky-blue; 'Persian Jewels' is a mixture of purples, pinks, blues and white.

Dwarf french marigolds, already mentioned, are half-hardy annuals, but if they are sown when the ground has warmed up, from late May onwards, they will flower where sown. The shorter varieties, like 'Dainty Marietta', 'Red Marietta', 'Goldrush', 'Boy O Boy' and 'Sparky' are the most suitable for this kind of situation.

Nasturtiums flower best on poor, dry, shallow soils; under better conditions they tend to produce too much leaf. 'Tom Thumb Mixed' are free-flowering on dwarf plants, 'Alaska' has white-marbled leaves.

Mignonette is grown not for its unexciting flowers but for the delicious scent, especially strong in the morning and evening.

Nemophila menziesii (baby blue eyes) is a carpeting annual with bell-shaped, sky-blue flowers with a white centre.

Phacelia campanularia, a similar but slightly taller plant, has bell-shaped blue flowers which are very attractive to bees.

Pheasant's eye (adonis) 'Scarlet Chalice' is a 12-inch (30 cm) tall annual which has been developed from the wild cornfield flower. It produces bright scarlet cup-shaped blooms with black centres, and dainty, fern-like foliage.

Swan River daisy (*Brachycome iberidifolia*), a neat little annual, flowers all summer in shades of mauve, blue, purple and white. The blooms are scented.

Ursinia anethoides has daisy-like, orange flowers zoned brownish-red in the centre, and feathery leaves. It flowers best in dry, sunny places.

Viscaria **'Rose Angel'** a pink-flowered dwarf annual, produces blooms only a few weeks after sowing and so is useful for quick effect.

Night-scented and Virginian stocks: I always recommend sowing these two plants together, as the Virginian Stock is an extremely pretty little flower – mainly pink and mauve, with some red, yellow and white mixed in – but it has no fragrance, while the night-scented stock looks nothing, but has one of the loveliest garden scents there are on warm evenings, especially before rain.

North- and east-facing walls and fences

The soil at the base of these walls is generally marginally damper than that near south- and west-facing walls, as the hot sun does not dry it out as much, but north- and east-facing walls can present a problem as they tend to lack sun and usually receive the brunt of cold northerly and easterly winds.

East-facing walls can be even more difficult than north ones as the very sun which helps to make them slightly warmer can be a particular drawback in early spring. While the sun in those early months is gaining strength rapidly, and rises progressively earlier, there can still be keen overnight frosts which reduce the temperature of the cell sap in the plants, and especially in any tender young shoots or flower buds which the warming sun may have encouraged to appear, to below freezing point. Frozen plant tissue in itself is not necessarily a bad thing, providing it is allowed to thaw out gradually, but the spring sun shining from the east melts the frozen sap rapidly. The cell walls cannot cope and are burst during the process. As a result young growth and leaf buds, early flowers and many types of evergreen leaves are killed off or severely browned, making the plant look sad and sorry, and, if it happens regularly, weakening it considerably or even finishing it off altogether.

If you intend to plant against an east-facing wall or fence, therefore, the plants you have to look for are deciduous ones which come into leaf or produce flowers later rather than earlier, or evergreens which have tough leaves rendering them impervious to this type of damage.

Lavender (*top left*) is excellent for hot, dry areas
Hebes (*top right*) on a warm, sunny bank
Hebe armstrongii (*bottom*) in a dry, sunny border
Dimorphotheca (*top left*), mesembryanthemum and portulaca (*bottom*) – three annuals which thrive in hot, dry places (*overleaf*)

Plants suitable for a north-facing wall or fence do not need to have these characteristics, but must be able to survive cold and often strong winds without browning or being weakened. Those suitable for both north and east aspects must either be able to support themselves efficiently, hang onto their supports tenaciously with tendrils or twining stems, or be rigid enough, with or without additional training, not to be battered to a pulp during periods of really strong wind.

As with all climbers and wall plants, it is essential that the soil should be in as good heart as possible, as it has to support plants of sometimes great height, and often during times of extreme dryness, when rain is blown against the back of the wall by south and west winds, leaving the soil dry at the front. Regular applications of organic material will keep the soil in good shape, and an occasional dressing with a high-potash fertilizer will toughen the tissue, which is important for plants growing in cold positions. It will also help to promote flowering. High-nitrogen fertilizers are not usually necessary, as they can encourage excessive, lush, flowerless growth which will be prone to frost damage.

Watch the level of moisture in the soil carefully when the plants are young, as if it dries out too much for too long your plants will fail to put on the amount of growth needed to cover a large proportion of the wall or fence in a reasonable time. You may also find that in the colder parts of the country you will need to protect very young specimens with hay or straw the first few winters after planting, although if you choose the right plants no further protection should be necessary after this time.

Wall plants can be prone to disease attack; the circulation of air necessary to disperse the spores will be absent, so the chances of their settling on the leaves in sufficient quantities to cause infection are greater. The most common disease is powdery mildew, which can be controlled in advance of attack by spraying the plant with Benlate or Dithane 945, and can even be cured to a large extent (if the infection

Scrophularia aquatica 'Variegata' and *Caltha palustris* 'Plena' both enjoy wet, sunny spots (*previous page*)
Nemophylla (*above left*) and limnanthes are suitable annuals for shallow soil
The author's cottage showing the narrow border where plants are growing in very shallow soil

is not too severe) with a preparation called Tumbleblite, containing the chemical propiconazole. This must not, however, be used on plants grown as food-crops.

In certain summers you could find your plants becoming infected with rust disease, which is more serious, and harder to deal with, but Tumbleblite has some effect. Scab can be a problem on certain plants, such as pyracantha, but it can be controlled with any of the products mentioned above. Roses growing against any aspect of wall or fence nearly always develop some black spot; again an approved fungicide like those listed here will control this, and a tar acid wash in winter should kill a lot of the overwintering spores.

Climbers and plants for training

Aristolochia macrophylla (Dutchman's pipe), a very vigorous climber, is not suitable for east walls as it can get frost-damaged, but will cover a large north aspect rapidly. It has huge, kidney- or heart-shaped leaves and unusual, pendulous, yellowish-green and brown flowers in July and August.

Camellias have the reputation for being tender, but *Camellia japonica* and its cultivars, which are the species hardiest in Britain, are as tough as laurel and will thrive in quite cold and sunless positions, providing the soil is acid and moist enough; if additional watering is necessary, rain or soft water should be used. East aspects are not as suitable as north as the early morning sun can scorch the flowers. Camellias are sturdy enough not to require support when planted against a wall. In limey areas they should be grown in large tubs containing an ericaceous compost (containing no lime or chalk).

Celastrus scandens, another very vigorous climber, is not grown for its small and insignificant flowers, but for its bright orange seed vessels and spectacular autumn colour.

Chaenomeles (formerly cydonia, often incorrectly called 'japonica') or flowering quinces will grow well on any aspect, including north and easterly ones. They are really free-standing shrubs but position and train well against a wall. *Chaenomeles japonica* is a smallish, thorny shrub with profuse, red, apple blossom-like flowers in spring, followed by edible quinces which are useful for jelly-making. *C. speciosa* has a more lax habit ideal for training. Recommended varieties are 'Moerloesii' (flowers apple-blossom pink outside, white inside); 'Simonii' (dark crimson); 'Nivalis' (white); 'Umbilicata' (salmon-pink). *C. superba* has a more bushy habit, and is not quite so good for training, but still makes an excellent specimen against a wall. The most widely available cultivars are 'Crimson and Gold', 'Firedance', 'Knaphill Scarlet' and 'Pink Lady'.

Clematis is such a large genus of plants that it would be difficult to go into the subject in detail in a book of this nature, but for anyone really 'hooked' on clematis there are many excellent publications around, including some of the detailed catalogues produced by the major clematis nurseries like Fisks of Westleton, Suffolk and Treasures of Tenbury, which in addition to listing a wide selection of plants also give experienced horticultural hints.

Clematis in general can be divided into two categories, the large-flowered hybrids and the smaller-flowered or 'wild' species. Nearly all clematis will grow on north and east walls, with the exception in cold or very exposed areas of evergreen forms such as *C. balearica* and *C. armandii*, which are slightly tender and also usually very early to flower. I also find that large-flowered hybrids flowering early in the summer are more suitable for north aspects than east ones because of frost damage, and double-flowering hybrids like 'Vyvyan Pennell' and the white 'Duchess of Edinburgh' are perhaps best avoided in less than perfect situations. Some really strong-growing species like *C. montana* and its various forms, and *C. viticella* and its cultivars, are prone to producing rampant growth rather than an abundance of flowers. In the main you will get a good display in the positions we are looking at with most other species, and some of the large-flowered hybrids retain their colour better if they are not in a very hot, sunny place. A good example of this is the popular 'Nellie Moser', pink with a deeper pink bar up the middle of the petals, which looks pale and 'washed out' unless planted in the shade.

In my own garden, I have a magnificent *C. montana* 'Rubens' which, although originally planted to cover two sides of an architecturally nondescript, flat-roofed extension in shade, has long since done its job in this respect and threatens to engulf the whole of the cottage. It is a delight in spring when completely smothered in pale pink, chocolate-scented flowers. There is also a first-class specimen of *C. alpina* growing over a pergola in shade which regularly produces masses of pendent, satin-blue flowers in April and May, and I am establishing a *C. jouiniana* in full, draughty shade at the back of the garage which is already giving a good display of massed blue, unusually-shaped flowers in autumn. The only disadvantage of this species is that it does not support itself with twining stems and leaves as other clematis do, needing to be tied to its trellis, but the effect is worth it. If you like unusual-looking forms, try C. *tangutica*, whose yellow, lantern-shaped flowers are followed by fluffy, old-man's-beard-like seed-heads enjoyed by many winter-visiting birds.

Large flowered forms which do well in my garden in either east or north facing positions are 'Gypsy Queen', which is a freer-flowering version of the lovely purple jackmanii; a good blue, 'William Kennett', which flowers twice, once in early summer, and then for a couple of months or so in autumn; the red-purple 'Rouge Cardinale'; the pink 'Hagley Hybrid' whose best aspect is north as it does not bleach so much and looks superb when in association with 'William Kennett'; and perhaps my all-time favourite, as it is hardly out of flower from early summer until the frosts and seems to be quite indestructible, the pink-mauve 'Comtesse de Bouchard'.

Perhaps a short word on cultivation would not come amiss here. The usual reasons for the failure of clematis are incorrect planting and clematis wilt. Clematis are lime-lovers, so it is doing them no favour at all to surround their roots on planting in a large quantity of peat. They are best in ordinary garden soil, which should be lightened with sharp sand if it is heavy and, if the ground is acid, the pH should be raised by liming. They should also be planted deeper than they were in the container, as they will form additional roots from the stem – one of the only times when this should be done on planting new stock. The roots must not be allowed to dry out, and feeding should be done annually, using a high-potash fertilizer with the addition of some magnesium: a rose food is suitable.

Clematis wilt is a disease which causes the plant to collapse and die in minutes. Not a lot is known about clematis wilt, but it has been discovered that if a plant should contract the disease, cut it down to ground level and water it with a fungicide such as Benlate, and it may re-grow.

Pruning clematis causes much anxiety, but is really quite simple. It is not necessary to prune most species at all unless they are getting into a tangle, in which case the cutting-back should be done immediately after flowering, with maybe another trim in the autumn – only do not cut back too hard late in the year or you will take off next year's flowering material. Early summer-flowering hybrids do not need much pruning, except to tidy them up occasionally and remove dead stems – this can be done after the first flush of flowers (many of them have a second flush in autumn). Hybrids flowering after midsummer can be cut down to the ground in spring – if they are not pruned at all they tend to produce all their flowers on long, bare stalks high up where they cannot be seen. Cutting the top third hard back, the centre third about half-way down, and leaving the last third unpruned will ensure a tall plant with plenty of leaves and flowers lower down.

Some **cotoneasters** are not quite as hardy as you would suppose, and can be browned in really cold winds. The three most reliable for north and east aspects are the deciduous *C. horizontalis*, and the two evergreens *C. lacteus* and *C. salicifolius floccosus*, which both produce large quantities of berries on a regular basis.

Escallonia is not suitable for east aspects, but will flower well if planted on the north side of a wall. The toughest forms are the two pink cultivars 'Edeniensis' and 'Donard Seedling'. Escallonias tend to lose their leaves in hard winters but new ones will appear when the weather warms up.

Euonymus fortunei varieties like those we have already looked at in connection with dry shade seem impervious to cold winds and frost, and many of them will climb slowly similarly to ivy, if planted against a wall. The best forms for this are 'Colorata', 'Silver Queen' ('Variegata'), and 'Vegetus'.

Forsythia suspensa is a lax-growing form of forsythia which

Forsythia suspensa

trains well. Better flowers are produced where the plant receives some sun, and the spring flowers are rarely browned by frost.

Garrya elliptica is a large shrub with leathery leaves and green catkins in winter, which are very popular with flower arrangers. The best catkins are found on male plants. Young garryas have something of a problem getting established on east-facing walls and fences because of spring frost damage, but this can be overcome in the early stages by 'lagging', as described above.

Nearly all varieties of **ledera** (ivy) are suitable, but the bright green ivy, *H. helix* 'Buttercup' loses its juvenile yellow foliage colour if it gets no sun at all. In really severe winters, *H. canariensis* 'Variegata' can be damaged by the cold, but once the plant is established, this should only be temporary. I have one on a north-east wall which is regularly wafted by breezes straight from the Urals in early spring, yet it puts on feet of growth every year.

Hydrangea petiolaris is self-supporting by means of aerial suckers and is best on a north or east wall, as a south or west one can be too hot. It can be a bit slow at the beginning, showing a reluctance to flower and climb by itself, but kept well watered it will eventually get going, hanging on strongly to any surface and producing large heads of white flowers in early summer.

The hardy **jasmines** are invaluable garden plants, growing and flowering well in most situations. *Jasminum nudiflorum*, the winter

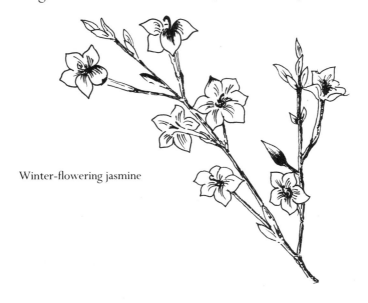

Winter-flowering jasmine

jasmine, has loose, green stems and yellow flowers in late winter and early spring. Pruning consists of cutting back to a main framework of mature, woody branches immediately after flowering. *Jasminum officinale*, the summer jasmine, is strong-growing, with white scented flowers for most of the summer. It flowers better where there is some sun, though this is not absolutely necessary for an adequate display. *Jasminum × stephanense* has pale pink scented flowers in July and August.

***Kerria japonica* 'Pleniflora'** is a tall, free-standing shrub with long green stems and leaves with serrated edges, which is covered with bright yellow, double flowers in spring and occasionally has another crop in autumn. It spreads by suckers. Very little pruning is necessary, other than removing unwanted suckers (which can be replanted elsewhere if required), trimming to shape, and cutting out dead stems which tend to build up inside the bush after a while.

The **honeysuckles** flower better if they receive sunshine for at least a part of the day, but they are woodland-fringe plants, so need a cool root run. For this reason, an east-facing wall is quite good, as the top growth will receive sun for part of the morning, but the roots are protected from the very hot south and west sunshine during summer. There are some forms which are all right when planted in full shade, including the one grown mainly for its golden variegated leaves, *Lonicera japonica* 'Aureo-reticulata'. *L. japonica* 'Halliana', another evergreen or semi-evergreen, will grow strongly and produce flowers in shade, as will the vigorous *L. × americana*, which has fragrant white flowers, turning yellow and then rose with age. The most suitable honeysuckles for an east aspect are the deciduous woodbines, *L. periclymenum* 'Belgica' (the early Dutch honeysuckle) and *L. periclymenum* 'Serotina' (the late Dutch honeysuckle). These have similarly shaped flowers, rose-purple on the outside and pale yellow on the inside of the lips, but the early Dutch honeysuckle flowers in May and June, and the late Dutch flowers from July to September. Honeysuckles support themselves by means of twining stems and therefore, like clematis, require some form of trellis or netting if they are to grow up a wall or fence.

The **parthenocissus** (ampelopsis) genus includes the much-loved Virginia creeper, *Parthenocissus quinquefolia*, which has five-lobed green leaves, turning bright red in autumn. Although partially self-clinging, this form is not very good at climbing and, in its youth especially, needs a lot of assistance to get started up a wall. Perhaps the best species of all is *P. henryana*, which climbs by both tendrils and adhesive pads. The leaves are three- and five-lobed, with veins picked out in pink and silver and, again, magnificent autumn colour, which lasts longer before the leaves drop if planted on a cooler aspect, although it will grow just about anywhere. 'Birch Grove Red' is a cultivar worth looking out for. The young leaves are tinted red, gradually turning dark green, and as it is not as strong a grower as other species it is useful for a more confined space.

Similar and closely related to the Virginia creepers are the **ornamental vines**. They, too, have brilliant autumn colour, but are perhaps more suitable for rambling through old trees than growing on walls, although if you have a large area to cover quickly, they can be just the job. *Vitis coignetiae* has enormous leaves and insignificant-looking though pleasantly scented clusters of flowers in summer, followed by small, purple grapes. *V. vinifera* 'Brandt' has edible, early-ripening, purple grapes. *V. vinifera* 'Purpurea' has very ornamental leaves which unfold red, turning purple as they mature.

Polygonum baldschuanicum (Russian, or mile-a-minute, vine) is wonderful for covering an eyesore in a season, but can quickly get out of hand if planted where space is limited or where it is not kept in check. In late summer it is almost hidden by a froth of creamy-white panicles turning pink as they mature. It can be cut back hard annually to keep it within bounds.

Pyracantha (firethorn) is a most accommodating genus of plants; they are quite undemanding as to their requirements and will therefore thrive on both north and east walls and fences, even in fairly poor soil. All pyracanthas produce berries ranging from bright yellow to intense red, following early summer heads of white, 'may-like' flowers. The most readily available from nurseries and garden centres are 'Mojave' (orange-red berries); 'Orange Charmer' (a viciously-spined, upright grower with vibrant orange berries); 'Orange Glow' (bright orange-red berries); *P. rogersiana* (red berries); *P. rogersiana*, 'Flava' (yellow berries); 'Soleil d'Or' (another yellow-berried cultivar which has a loose, spreading habit excellent for training); 'Teton' (another upright form, but with small leaves and yellow-orange berries); and 'Waterii' (bright red berries). I have all these growing on various easterly and northern aspects, where they thrive, regardless of the wind from the Urals and the occasional dousing of salty water in winter from the road that runs alongside.

All the plants described above are purely ornamental ones which will tolerate colder and sunless walls; apart from the ornamental vine 'Brandt' and the flowering quinces, they are food for the soul only. However, there are certain wall plants which both look decorative and produce fruit which is palatable as well. One of these is the **morello cherry**, which is covered in white cherry-blossom in spring, followed in most years by an enormous crop of acid cherries which are excellent for pies, jam-making, freezing and wine. It is quite happy on a north wall, but on an east-facing one the flowers can be nipped by a late frost. A fan-trained morello cherry needs plenty of space to develop, but makes a good disguise for a blank wall.

Then there is the **blackberry**, and also hybrid berries which are usually some form of cross between a blackberry and a raspberry. Blackberries will fruit well on either a north or an east wall; hybrid berries like the **loganberry** and **tayberry** are better on an east wall where they will receive some sun to ripen the berries. 'Bedford Giant' is a reliable variety of blackberry, which is a strong grower producing heavy crops of large, early-ripening fruit. A more decorative variety is the 'Oregon Thornless', a type of parsley-leaved blackberry, which is less rampant than most and so handy for small gardens. 'Merton Thornless' is another thorn-free form with good crops of fruit in August and September.

The loganberry has red fruit in July and August like a large, rather acid raspberry. The tayberry produces longer, sweeter fruit of a dark red which is almost purple when fully ripe, at about the same time. The best way to train these berries on a wall is to stretch wires along it at about 2 feet (60 cm) spacings above the ground. The new canes formed during the summer are trained upwards in the centre of the plant; after flowering, the old canes are cut out and the new ones, thinned if there are too many, are trained fan-wise, leaving the middle of the bush open, so that there is somewhere to tie the new canes temporarily the following season until they are trained in to replace those which have fruited that year, and so on.

The majority of **roses** do not take kindly to sunless or very chilly locations, so they really should not be the first choice when considering planting up a northerly or eastern aspect, but if you are desperate to plant some and these are the only positions available, there are a limited number of climbers which will put up a reasonable performance when faced with such a situation. Those easiest to obtain and cultivate are as follows:

Danse du Feu: Red, scentless. Needs preventive spraying for mildew.
Etoile de Holland: Red, heavily scented. May need preventive spraying for disease.
Gloire de Dijon: Buff-orange with yellow and apricot. 'Tea' scented.
Golden Showers: Golden yellow, scented. Healthy but moderate grower.

Climbing rose 'Golden Showers'

Guinee: Deep scarlet, scented.
Madame Alfred Carrière: Strong-growing, pink-budded, white rose. Light green foliage prone to mildew in certain seasons.
Madame Gregoire Staechelin: Deep pink, heavily scented. Very beautiful in June and July but sadly not repeat-flowering.
Maigold: Golden yellow, healthy, fragrant.
Parkdirektor Riggers: Blood red, semi-double, vigorous.

As with all climbing roses trained on a wall or fence, the branches should be trained out as near horizontally as possible. This promotes the production of short stems terminating in flower buds from the leaf joints, which in turn prevents all the flowers from being formed at the top of the plant, and also keeps the climbing rose at a more manageable height.

The narrow passage

This is not an easy part of the garden, but one which seems to be on the increase with modern housing development as more and more detached homes are crammed onto an acre, even if they are only 'detached' by enough ground to allow a person to walk from front to back. With new homes the 'side garden' is very much a thing of the past, unless you manage to get hold of a corner plot. What has taken its place is a cold, draughty passage, often sunless, with maybe a concrete path occupying over half of it.

This kind of situation is almost as hopeless to deal with as the impossible spot described in the Introduction on page 7 – but not quite as bad, as in that instance nearly every cultural difficulty had gathered together. At least with most passages between houses and bungalows there is light at either end and a sound gutter to prevent the constant drip from the roof onto the plants below.

The difficulties which *do* confront one where properties are very close together are mainly lack of light, draughts and cold, and shortage of space. If the amount of bare earth is very small the tidiest answer might be to gravel the area, making a feature of such things as side doors by planting a topiary box clipped into a pyramid shape in a good-looking tub and placing this to one side. I have had one for many years in a cold, sunless place and it is quite happy. The side passage is not, however, the part of the garden where you put all your undisguised bags of rubbish, dead houseplants, surplus plastic plant-pots and the rusting garden roller. I am firmly of the belief that any situation should be made the best of, and, as I have said before, there is usually some way you can introduce improvements.

Where the path does not go right up to the house wall, or if you can manage to break out a hole or remove half a slab, the starkness of the area can be softened by growing something up the wall. You need something bright, self-clinging to hold its own against the amount of wind it will receive, tough because that wind will be very cold and strong at times, unoffended if you forget to water it, not likely to lose its colour if it receives no sun, and narrow of habit so it does not decrease the width of the passage any more than is necessary and will not obstruct the path. I cannot think of a better choice than the form of the common ivy with a bright yellow centre to its green leaves – *Hedera helix* 'Gold-heart'. It clings strongly, grows quickly, and if the odd stem starts growing away from the wall, it can be cut off without spoiling anything. Even if you plant nothing else in that spot, as long as you keep the paving or gravelled surfaces tidy, you will probably need nothing else in order to make things look 100 per cent better.

There is often a further complication with a passage between two properties in that the side doors might be facing each other, and there is frequently a desire between neighbours for privacy. If there is nothing in the deeds to prevent it, the best screening is generally afforded by erecting a low wooden fence, which, although not giving total privacy, creates the impression that you have the protection of your own garden around you! A substantial trellis can give the same feeling, or, if you know a handyman or you are not too concerned about cost, a more substantial substitute is the pierced-screen or honeycomb wall, again making sure you do not compound the problem by having it too tall.

Hedges

There is the alternative of planting a hedge, although more complications arise if you opt for this method of dividing two properties. It must not grow so quickly that it is capable of getting out of hand and annoying both you and the neighbours, it should be suitable for clipping into a fairly narrow section so that it does not unduly encroach on the already limited space, and it must be able to stand cold and wind. As you can imagine, the choice is limited, but there are a few of which I have personal knowledge that will fit into this category.

The first is **field maple** *(Acer campestre)* which makes an excellent hedge as well as a brightly coloured autumn tree, but cannot be clipped too narrow. You may find that the leaves will not colour up as well in a sunless position and, being deciduous, it could cause annoyance to neighbours when the leaves are shed over autumn and winter.

Another native tree which also makes an indestructible hedge is **quickthorn** *(Crataegus monogyna)*. Much of what has been said about field maple equally applies to quickthorn, but it will trim to a fairly narrow form and it has the advantage of thorns – useful if next-door's dog is not your cup of tea, but not so useful when the toddler falls into it!

Beech (*Fagus sylvatica*) makes a lovely hedge for most positions and at any height; although if you have difficult soil you might consider planting **hornbeam** (*Carpinus betulus*) instead. The drawback with these is again one of leaf-shedding – although deciduous beech tends to retain the dead leaves throughout winter and so can cause much irritation because, unlike most deciduous bushes, you cannot have one or two good clean-ups and get the job over with for the year.

A very effective partition for such a situation, especially if there is a post-and-wire fence between the gardens, is **pyracantha**, trained along the wires and supported by the posts. This makes a very narrow espalier which is pruned by removing all unwanted new growths after the plants have flowered, and periodically for the rest of summer when more growth should appear. This method of training ensures a lot of berries, even in the less-than-perfect position of a narrow passage.

If, like me, you cannot bear to leave any potentially useful piece of ground unplanted, there are some plants which will give good decorative effect to the rest of the area. What you are looking for is something fairly low, otherwise it may get in the way, well-shaped and interesting, as it is often the first area one notices when walking to the back of the property, and tolerant of both cold and, generally, shade. It is also a good idea to plant something tough and taller at the windy end of the passage to form a slight wind-break. Suitable plants for this are *Elaeagnus ebbingei*, sea buckthorn (*Hippophae rhamnoides*) and *Cotoneaster simonsii*.

Herbaceous perennials

Ajuga (see page 26).

Alchemilla mollis will grow almost anywhere, although its green sprays of tiny flowers are more subtle than exciting. This plant may seed rather too well in good soil.

Anemone nemorosa (woodland anemone) will succeed on both heavy and light soils and flowers for a long period in spring. The variety 'Alba Plena' has pure white, double flowers.

Bergenia (see page 39)

Brunnera (see page 40). *B. macrophylla* 'Variegata' should not be planted as it is not tough enough for these conditions.

Geranium endressii **'Wargrave Pink'**. Nearly all hardy geraniums would produce a good splash of colour, but this species is particularly popular, as it is easy to grow and very bright, with a long flowering season. *Geranium himalayense* 'Plenum' is also very useful, both for its neat foliage and for its lavender-blue double flowers, again produced over several months.

Ompalodes verna (blue-eyed Mary), a low-growing, blue-flowered plant; makes a forget-me-not-like show in spring. 'Alba' is a pretty white form.

Pulmonaria (see page 41)

Saxifraga fortunei is a rockery-type plant, which has white flowers in autumn. There are two purple-leaved forms – *S. rubrifolia*, which is coppery-coloured, and 'Wada's Variety', with rich purple leaves.

Soldanella villosa produces dainty, lavender-blue flowers and looks good as an edging to a path.

Tiarella cordifolia has maple-like leaves and white flower spikes. It makes an attractive mixture with *Heuchera* **'Bressingham Hy-brids '** which has similarly shaped foliage and sprays of pink and red flowers in early summer, and with *Tellima grandiflora* **'Purpurea'** . There is a cross between heuchera and tiarella, *Heucherella* **'Briget Bloom'** which has light pink flower spikes and should grow in the sort of spot we are looking at providing the soil is light.

Symphytum grandiflorum 'Variegatum' should be included in this kind of area if at all possible, not so much for its rather insignificant pink comfrey flowers but for its bright gold-variegated leaves, which do not seem to be affected by any adversity.

Shrubs

Berbis stenophylla **'Corallina Compacta'** is a very dwarf, slow-growing berberis with tiny, narrow, evergreen leaves and yellow flowers in summer. Many other berberis would succeed in this area, but some may get too big. If there is a path, it is important that varieties are chosen which will not spread too far, and they should be planted well away from the path edge, if only for the sake of any nylon tights which may be passing that way!

Cornus canadensis (creeping dogwood) is easy to grow

providing the soil is not alkaline. It spreads by means of suckering stems and has pure white flowers in summer, followed by red berries.

Euonymus fortunei varieties (see page 44). Those which climb slowly, as described under plants for north and east walls, would also be suitable for covering a solid wall or fence between two properties, as they can be kept in bounds.

Most of the prostrate and low-growing forms of **cotoneaster** would grow quite happily, even under really difficult conditions, in the gap between two properties. Look out for *C. humifusus* 'Oakwood', which is a tidier version of the plant *humifusus,* also known as *C. dammeri.* It is very prostrate, rooting where it touches, with small, bluish-green leaves and red berries. It does not spread as rapidly as *C. dammeri. C. microphyllus* forms hummocks, which are covered in autumn with large, crimson berries.

Hypericum prolificum flowers better with some sun, but will tolerate partial shade and does not seem to mind draught. It has a bushy, rounded habit, narrow, shiny, green leaves and clusters of yellow flowers all summer.

Ilex crenata **'Convexa'** looks more like box than holly. It is a dense bush, spreading about 30 inches (80 cm) and growing about as tall, with small, wavy-edged leaves and black berries.

The prostrate members of the **rubus** family, *Rubus calycinioides* and *R. tricolor*, are perhaps too far-reaching for many passages between houses, and may stray unwantedly onto your neighbour's property. However, if you just want to cover the whole area as quickly as

Rubus tricolor

possible with something evergreen which looks reasonable, these might be the plants for you.

Weigela **'Evita'** is a newish introduction, a dwarf form of an unexacting shrub but one which would normally be too bushy for most narrow passages. It is handy for an area where it will be seen quite a lot as it has a much longer flowering season than most weigelas.

Conifers

You have to be careful when choosing conifers for a spot between two houses as many of them, particularly chamaecyparis, would resent the draught and, if sun were lacking, golden-leaved conifers would turn green. However, some prostrate and semi-prostrate conifers would survive reasonably well here, and are worth mixing with other plants to give a variation in form and texture.

Abies balsamea **'Nana'** is a slow-growing 'fir' with a rounded habit and dark green needles. It has prominent winter buds which give it interest.

Juniperus horizontalis seems to shrug off most adversity, and there are many cultivars to choose from these days. Quite a few, like 'Banff', 'Blue Chip', 'Glauca', 'Hughes', and 'Turquoise Spreader' have blue, grey or glaucous foliage, which colours better in fairly good light. 'Prince of Wales' is a green, ground-hugging form which does not get too large for a confined space.

Microbiota decussata has lacy green foliage, a low, spreading habit, and the additional advantage of turning a bronze colour in winter. It makes an interesting change from some of the better known conifers.

Picea omorika **'Nana'** is a small, Christmas tree-shaped conifer, but with blue-green undersides to the needles. In my garden, it occupies a very draughty spot without turning a hair (or needle, perhaps) and does not seem to mind being overhung by other shrubs.

Pinus leucodermis and its dwarf cultivars are trouble-free 'pines'. They have very dark green needles which are very shiny and seem to be able to tolerate a fairly heavy soil.

There are a few forms of **yew**, with prostrate or semi-prostrate

A shady corner of the author's garden under an apple tree

Prunus lusitanica 'Variegata' growing in dry shade

habit, which could be used in this situation. *Taxus baccata* 'Repandans' is a small conifer with long, spreading branches, drooping at the tips. 'Repens Aurea' is quite prostrate, with leaves margined with yellow when young, turning cream later. 'Semperaurea' is more erect, but wide-spreading and not a fast grower, which could be planted where space is not too tight.

There are one or two semi-prostrate forms of the **eastern hemlock (tsuga)** which should survive in this type of area, especially if the draught is broken a little with other, tougher plants. The ones most easy to obtain are the semi-prostrate 'Bennett' and 'Jeddeloh' and the prostrate 'Cole'. These conifers are a bit more special, but if you pass this particular part of the garden a great deal, they may be worth considering.

Climbers

I know many people who try to grow something on the fence between two houses, and are frequently not successful. The two things to remember are: don't try to be too ambitious; and not everyone likes the same plants as you (or, indeed, any plants at all!) so don't assume that your neighbour wants creepers wandering into his or her garden.

I have already suggested *Euonymus fortunei* as being suitable for a solid wooden fence; where the fence is open-work, or you have a pierced screen wall, you really need something more twining, but which does not get out of hand. **Clematis** is the obvious choice, but you need a pretty tough one to give a really good display in the teeth of a howling, funnelled gale. My old favourite, 'Comtesse de Bouchard' (see page 94) fits the bill admirably, is unfussy about situation, and if trimmed back to any height, it will always grow to about 10 feet (3 metres), then stop and produce a profusion of flower buds, so it can be trained along the wall or fence without getting out of hand. 'Horn of Plenty' is a strong grower, with lavender-rose flowers and purple stamens. In good conditions it will cover a large area, but, faced with the adversity we are looking at, it should make good growth and flower well without getting out of hand, and can be cut back to ground level in spring to keep it within bounds.

Sempervivum flourishing without soil on a pantiled roof
Ruta **'Jackman's Blue' likes a hot, dry site**

'Jackmanii Superba' is an all-time favourite, with purple flowers and a very accommodating habit; in the situation we are facing it should do well without putting on unwanted growth.

Few neighbours could object to sweet-smelling plants grown on their boundary which might intrude, so **honeysuckle** becomes an obvious choice. *Lonicera periclymenum* 'Belgica' and 'Serotina' are capable of being trimmed back if they exceed the space provided. If you have a really difficult place, where the soil is poor and there is a lot of shade, try *Lonicera caprifolium* (early cream honeysuckle), with grey-green leaves, heavily scented, creamy-white flowers with pink tints in high summer, followed by orange-red berries, which will germinate readily if sown into good seedling compost and produce plants of a very passable quality.

Salt-affected areas

A few years ago the only places in Britain likely to be seriously affected by salt were coastal areas. Here the soil would contain a high concentration of salt, and winds off the sea would be regularly laced with saline spray. This resulted in a particular maritime flora, the plants not only tolerating salt, but positively revelling in it.

The increasing use of salt on our roads in winter to prevent and clear the build-up of ice and snow has resulted in a new type of environment developing, not dissimilar from that of the coastal region, especially adjacent to our busier roads where the plants are regularly lashed by salty water in winter, and the soil becomes more 'coastal' with regard to the salt content with every winter that passes. It is interesting to note that uncultivated roadside verges and central reservations are beginning to sport a maritime flora of their own, helped a great deal by the lorries making regular trips to the ports, where seeds of salt-loving plants picked up on the wheels and the vehicle undersides drop off at random and are dispersed throughout the country.

Left to its own devices, nature has a great talent for adaptation, but where interference is desired, for example if we should want to create a garden under such circumstances, then we have to emulate this natural adjustment and use plants which are not going to object to salty soil and salty water. Salt is highly toxic to many species – it can even be used as a weedkiller between paving stones. On the other hand, unless you actually live on the marshes or the dunes, it is unlikely that the whole garden will be seriously affected by salt; the problem area will be that which is immediately next to a heavily salted road or facing the sea without protection from salt-laden gales. When you are designing the garden, therefore, your main objective should be to create a salt-tolerant barrier between the source of the trouble – road or sea – which will grow well under such conditions and so look presentable, while protecting the rest of the garden to enable a wider range of plants to be grown.

Of course, the easiest way to do this, but certainly not the most attractive, is to erect a tall fence or wall. Unfortunately, though, this can sometimes be less than totally effective as during periods of strong wind, the down-draughts produced by the barrier on its leeward side can carry some salt over it which will affect the plants on the other side. If a living screen is used, it is more likely to filter and absorb the salty wind so the plants the other side will be unaffected.

More than any other, this situation calls for a good imagination. As I write this, it is a lovely day in early autumn, and along the main road on the edge of our village, where new properties are springing up like mushrooms in this season of mists and mellow fruitfulness, excited gardeners are installing miles of Leyland cypress, laurel, beech and thuya. It is hard to believe that in a couple of months or so the heat shimmering on the road will be replaced with brown, salty slush, most of which will be hurled relentlessly at these carefully planted young hedges.

It never ceases to surprise me how unobservant we can be; if one were to stand by these new hedges and look at the mature properties to left, right and over the other side of the road, the prospect is much less joyful: mature beech hedges gradually sickening as the salt in the soil builds up, defoliated laurel bushes with only a few yellowing leaves still putting up a fight on the tallest tips of the branches; one-sided Leyland cypress screens where the whole of the hedge on the roadside has been completely killed with salt spray, thuya with no bottom greenery at all. These are hedges of many years' growth which are strong enough to fight off the problem somewhat, even though the results are far from pretty. Young plants just do not stand a chance. What a pity we do not use our eyes more and look into the problem properly before wasting so much time and money, and so many beautiful young plants.

I am as guilty as anyone. A few years ago, when I went to live on the north Lincolnshire coast, I was initially delighted to have half an acre after the two years of 'back yard' gardening previously described. The size of the garden must have gone to my head, as I did not notice the heavy clay, high brackish water-table, and howling, salty, easterly winds until it was too late to retreat. I suppose we are all guilty of trying to rush things; all my favourites were lovingly introduced in no time at all. As I have mentioned before, even though the east coast climate seems inclement, the temperature is much more even than further inland and nearly always a few degrees higher overall in winter. This results in an early showing of new growth. But with the spring come the on-shore winds, and the whole lot is decimated.

I soon realized that I had been trying to run before I could walk, and promptly erected a shelter belt of *Sorbus intermedia* (Swedish whitebeam), *Populus alba* (white poplar) and *Salix alba* (white willow), interplanted with *Hippophae rhamnoides* (see buckthorn) and *Pinus maritima* (Corsican pine). Unfortunately, circumstances necessitated yet another move before I could enjoy the results of my labours, but I understand that, provided you do not mind good hard work on the clay, this particular garden is one of the best in the district for growing just about anything, now that the salt spray is unable to penetrate further than the shelter belt. It seems to be that, as far as soil salt concentration is concerned, most plants are capable of tolerating a great deal, as the high salty water table seems to have little effect there on the majority of common species, which goes to show just how much salt is pumped into our main road verges every year for it to have such a detrimental effect on so many things.

The species most likely to succeed where a lot of salt is being thrown about are, in general, deciduous (so the salt settles on the dormant branches and not on the leaves, which often burn) and fairly deep-rooted (so the feeding roots are not damaged and do not absorb too much salt). Some evergreens can be temporarily browned, resulting in an overwinter loss of leaves, but this is usually rectified in spring with a new flush.

At my present property, plants I find will put up with an odd dose of salty water are *Ligustrum ovalifolium* (hedging privet), pyracantha – though this can suffer some die-back to the tips – and *Cotoneaster horizontalis,* but I would stress that these are planted where the road is salted perhaps only two or three times a winter, and I doubt if they would tolerate much more than this. Until recently there was also a 30-year-old *Laburnum vossii* in the same area, which grew and flowered magnificently, despite receiving the salty run-off from the road. It was showing signs of approaching departure in the heartwood, but I put this down more to the fact that the poor thing was concreted up to the trunk (not by me!) and laburnum in general is not a long-lived tree.

I also find that the smaller and narrower the leaf, the more likely a plant is to withstand salt in the wind. Pines, with their tough, leathery needles, will cope with airborne salt well, provided there is not too much build-up in the soil. As well as the Corsican pine, our native *Pinus sylvestris* (Scots pine), should also survive without showing signs of stress, but I find that the needles of many firs (picea) seem to be rather soft and can brown in severe conditions, although new growth will appear at the ends of the branches in spring. However, although this is acceptable for forestry purposes, it is unsightly in the ornamental garden, and therefore this species is best avoided. Most ornamental conifers, for example junipers, cypress, and chamaecyparis, brown at the first hint of salt, and are useless as the first line of defence against salty winds.

If you have an open-plan frontage, I find a temporary solution to salt spray is summer bedding plants. Most common species do not seem to be affected by moderate amounts of salt in the soil, and planting a bright display in summer is more aesthetic than a row of sickly perennial subjects. Winter is more of a problem, as most of the winter bedding plants – wallflowers, forget-me-nots, Canterbury bells and 'Universal' pansies – can be severely damaged by salt spray.

The lack of flowers can be overcome by planting many of the spring-flowering bulbs, which appear to be reasonably unaffected by salt, especially those which can be planted fairly deep, like daffodils, tulips, bluebells and even crocuses. This should leave only a month or two when the soil is bare.

A rather bizarre alternative is to plant the ornamental kale. Most brassicas (members of the cabbage family) enjoy a high proportion of salt in the soil, but unless you like sprouts in your front garden you could consider this ornamental relative, which looks rather like an open savoy and has leaves variegated in pink, cream and green, with purple tinges – not to everyone's taste but certainly capable of creating a talking point!

A tip for anyone who lives on a roadside not normally affected by salt but whose plants receive a 'one-off' dose from an over-zealous gritter is to hose down the affected ones as soon as possible after the attack (not while the weather is very cold, of course, or any water running onto the road or pavement could turn into a skating-rink!).

Herbaceous perennials
(For areas where a salt barrier is impossible or undesirable.)

The common sea lavender (**Limonium vulgare**) is found in large

116

amounts on salt marshes. There are some very attractive garden cultivars, like the dwarf *L. incanum dumosum,* with pink flower heads which are excellent for drying. Another good dried flower is *L. incanum* 'Violette'; a violet-blue sea lavender which keeps its colour for ages when dried.

The well-known **Oenothera biennis** (evening primrose) is really a biennial. It is naturalized on sand dunes and grows in perpetuity in the majority of gardens because of the large amount of seed it produces. It grows to about 3 feet (1 metre) and has large yellow flowers which open in the evening and are attractive to night-flying moths. Each flower lasts only a day, but is succeeded by many others. There are many perennial garden cultivars, like *O. glaber* (compact, with bronzy-green foliage); 'Highlight'; *O. linearis;* and the prostrate *O. missouriensis.*

Lupinus arboreus (tree lupin) is a short-lived shrubby perennial which originally came to the British Isles in the eighteenth century from California and is now naturalized on dunes and wasteland near the sea. It grows to 10 feet (3 metres) and has yellow, lupin-like flowers which are sometimes variegated.

Saxifraga rosacea (Irish saxifrage) looks similar to many of the mossy saxifrages but it is highly tolerant of salt. It is not easily acquired but can be obtained from specialist alpine nurseries and firms dealing in indigenous plant species.

Armeria (thrift, sea pink), a low-growing plant which makes excellent ground cover if mass-planted and will add interest to a roadside verge. It has dense 'mossy' foliage and pink flowers which have a flush in late spring and early summer and tend to be produced thereafter spasmodically until the autumn. *A. maritima* is the common wild pink, and it has good garden forms like 'Alba' (white), 'Dusseldorf Pride' (deep pink, almost red), and 'Ruby Glow'. *A. caespitosa* is a very dwarf, rockery species, which also has good modern cultivars like the bright pink 'Bevan's Beauty'.

The common sea holly, **Eryngium maritimum**, is found on many of the sand dunes in Britain, and has given rise to some of our most useful and adaptable plants. *E. planum* is a good deep blue which is useful in flower arrangements. *E. variifolium* has attractive, evergreen, marbled leaves. *E. giganteum* 'Miss Wilmott's Ghost' is a free-seeding biennial which has silver flower heads and silvery-green foliage. It is a striking plant in the right situation but as its seedlings spring up everywhere it can become a nuisance.

For anyone who has a serious salt problem, it may be an idea to establish so-called 'wild' maritime species, like sea stock *(Matthiola sinuata)*, sea spurge *(Euphorbia paralias)*, sea sandwort *(Honkenya peploides)*, sea bindweed *(Calystegia soldanella)*, sea rocket *(Calkile maritima)*, sea campion *(Silene maritima)*, sea pea *(Lathyrus japonicus)*, oysterplant *(Mertensia maritima)*, and reflexed stonecrop *(Sedum reflexum)*. Specialist wild flower seed producers like Johnsons of Boston, Lincolnshire, and John Chambers of Barton Seagrave, Northamptonshire, should be able to advise on this subject.

Roses

Many of the old-fashioned species roses, like *Rosa moyesii*, the bluish-leaved *R. rubrifolia*, the flamboyant-thorned *R. sericea* var. *pteracantha* and the grey-green leaved *R. willmottiae* seem to stand reasonable amounts of salt. There is a hedge of *R. rugosa* fronting a very busy main road near us which flourishes in spite of heavy

Sweetbriar

lashings of salt water in winter, and even hedges of stronger-growing floribundas, like 'Queen Elizabeth', and hybrid musks such as the cream 'Prosperity' and apricot 'Buff Beauty' appear to take some salt in their stride.

Two species of rose are particularly obliging when it comes to salt: *R. pimpinellifolia* (the Scotch or burnet rose) and *R. rubignosa* (sweet briar). The burnet rose produces a spiny thicket of branches and large, single, white or, infrequently, pale pink flowers, followed by blackish-red hips. The variety *R. pimpinellifolia harisoni* has double, scented, sulphur-yellow flowers. 'Stanwell Perpetual' is a perpetual-flowering, pale pink form with greyish leaves.

The sweet briar, or eglantine, has dainty buds and small, single, pink flowers followed by bright red hips. The foliage is richly fragrant and can be smelled whenever a breeze disturbs it.

Trees and shrubs

The most effective maritime planting I have ever seen was on the north Norfolk coast, where a holiday house had been built in the 1930s fronting onto the sand dunes, in a position where planning permission would be virtually unobtainable today. The front garden was literally part of the dunes, and was almost pure sand. At high tide it ran the risk of being totally submerged, salty winds swept the area nearly all the year round, and if you licked your fingers after you had weeded the garden, they tasted more salty than if you had just consumed a packet of salt and vinegar crisps! The planting, like Topsy, had just 'grow'd' over the years by a succession of owners: what survived flourished and what did not disappeared fairly rapidly.

The plants that thrived were allowed more or less to naturalize, and comprised the versatile yellow Spanish broom (*Spartium junceum*), assorted genistas, the grey-leaved *Senecio* 'Sunshine', various dwarf spiraeas, especially *S.* 'Goldflame' (see page 67) and *S.* 'Anthony Waterer' and *Rubus calyciniodes* as ground cover, all mixed up with young sea buckthorn plants. Hardly any maintenance was necessary, other than trimming over from time to time to keep the plants in shape.

I have already mentioned that shrubs which have few conventional leaves are more likely to survive a salty onslaught than the general run of plants. Spartium and genista come into this category, of course, and so do the true brooms, cytisus, and gorse (ulex). Tamarisk is another group which, because of its small, feathery foliage, is able to face up to salt spray. The common tamarisk, *Tamarix gallica,* has become naturalized in many maritime areas; it grows about 10 feet (3 metres) tall and has pink flowers throughout the second half of summer. *T. pentrandra* and its cultivars 'Pink Cascade' and 'Rubra' are very attractive shrubs, but not quite as good at withstanding the full force of salty wind; *T. tetrandra,* which flowers earlier in the year, is slightly better at this.

Hippophae rhamnoides (sea buckthorn) can be seen growing wild in great profusion along many of the coastal stretches of Britain, but it makes a superb informal hedge where much salt is present, filtering most of the salt so it does not blow inside the garden. Sea buckthorn has willowy grey leaves and dark stems covered in vicious spines, and the female plants produce bright orange berries in late summer and autumn.

Our two native viburnums – *V. opulus* (guelder rose) and *V. lantana* (wayfaring tree) have normal leaf forms but are extremely tolerant of a wide range of conditions and, being deciduous, will shrug off salt

Viburnum lantana

with ease. They make useful berrying hedges or individual shrubs where many other species would often get seriously damaged.

Some leathery-leaved evergreens will survive salt spray, or are capable of shedding badly affected foliage and producing new leaves in spring without detrimental effect. *Elaeagnus ebbingei* and *E. commutata* come into this group. Holly (ilex) will also put up with a great deal, as does *Garrya elliptica*, and aucuba. In maritime areas, slightly less hardy evergreens such as the grey, holly-leaved *Olearia macrodonta*, which has white, daisy-like flowers in summer, escallonia, *Choisya ternata*, some cotoneasters and the easily recognized *Eucalyptus gunnii* can be planted without fear of damage, but inland the combination of lower temperatures, icy-cold winds and the salt-laden traffic wash is likely to prove too much for them.

There are other tough, 'cheap-and-cheerful' shrubs which can be employed as a screen to protect less adaptable plants. *Sambucus nigra* (elder) and its ornamental cultivars will survive all but the heaviest concentrations of salt. *Ribes sanguineum* (flowering currant) is virtually indestructible, as are symphoricarpos (snowberry) and *Cornus sanguinea*. Most hypericums are impervious to salt and the many cultivars of *Buddleia davidii* also seem to cope well.

Trees

As far as trees are concerned, those which survive under these conditions are often more suited to parkland than limited suburban gardens and seaside plots, but where space will permit, they can be used effectively as protection for the rest of the site. I have already mentioned white poplar and willow in connection with a garden of my own; instead of the Swedish whitebeam, or, indeed, as well as it if I had had the room, I could have used one of the other whitebeams, such as *Sorbus aria* 'Lutescens', *S.* × 'Magnifica' or *S.* 'Mitchellii'. Where space is at a premium, the small *S.* × *hostii* comes in useful, perhaps for planting on a verge.

Most forms of hawthorn (crataegus) will tolerate salt, both in the soil and in the wind. I have described some of the most attractive garden forms on page 43, and it should not be forgotten that quickthorn hedging is one of the most versatile that one can plant as it is inexpensive, as tough as old boots, fast growing and eventually almost impenetrable. (Another salt-tolerant hedge can be made from *Berberis thunbergii* and its various cultivars, both green-leaved and purple. It will also provide an effective animal-proof barrier in a very short time.

Hawthorn flowers

For an informal garden, *Prunus spinosa* (blackthorn) can be trained into a moderate-sized tree which will not be damaged by salt, and it will be especially appreciated by lovers of sloe gin! Blackthorn will also clip as a hedge, and mixes well with quickthorn to make an attractive barrier for a rural setting.

Acer campestre, our native field maple, also makes a reasonable-sized tree, with the most delightful autumn colour and, like blackthorn and quickthorn, can be used for hedging, either on its own or mixed with these other species.

Many of the other acers are also salt-tolerant. Where there is plenty of space and a serious salt problem, one could not do much better than plant the ubiquitous sycamore, *Acer pseudoplatanus.* This has many attractive smaller-growing forms which are ideal for roadside planting, as the salt spray problem has usually disappeared by the time the leaves come out in spring, but they are not as suitable for maritime areas where there is a chance of salty winds even in the summer, as these can damage the less tough variegated or coloured leaves which several cultivars sport. Among the names to look out for

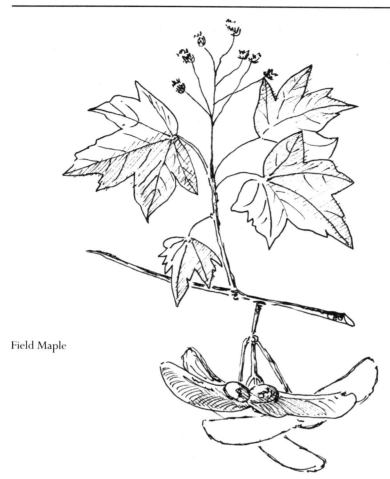

Field Maple

where an inland garden is concerned are 'Leopoldii' (yellowish-pink leaves speckled white); 'Spaethii' (the purple sycamore), and 'Worleei' (the golden sycamore). The Norway maple (*Acer platanoides*) can also be planted in these situations; again, the plain green forms tend to withstand summer salt winds better than the coloured ones like 'Drummondii' (variegated green and cream), 'Goldsworth Purple' and 'Royal Red'.

Another tree which makes a good maritime subject, although it can be much less satisfactory in cold areas inland, is the holm or evergreen oak, *Quercus ilex*. This has medium-sized, holly-shaped leaves and in time it forms a dense head. It is yet another species which will form a hedge if close-planted and clipped into shape regularly.

For sites which are subjected to light salt spray some way inland from the sea, but where the soil is not affected, the birches are a good choice. Varieties of our native silver birch, *Betula pendula*, are the easiest to grow, but should not be planted too near the coast, as salty spring winds are likely to destroy any new leaves which have appeared. The forms of birch with very spectacular bark, such as *B. costata*, *B. ermanii*, *B. jaqumontii* and *B. utilis* are also worth a try. I have, however, found that salty run-off from roads can affect young birches detrimentally, and so they are perhaps not such a good choice for inland salty sites.

Ash is a similar tree, in that it is less affected by salty winds than saline run-off. Most ash are far too big for the average garden, but *Fraxinus excelsior* 'Jaspidea' (the golden ash) makes a much smaller tree, with soft yellow young leaves turning light green as they mature, then colouring again in autumn before they fall. The wood is yellow, and is particularly attractive when seen against a winter sky.

Vandal-affected areas

Vandals come in all shapes and sizes. The most popular picture of the vandal is the bored youngster with no beauty in his or her soul, who has an incomprehensible urge to destroy anything that has some attractiveness about it. A trail of uprooted or snapped-off plants usually follows in his wake, and he enjoys a great feeling of vindictive satisfaction at the results.

However, vandals can also have four legs, and range in height from a few inches to several feet. Probably one of the most destructive is the rabbit, which seems to have an insatiable appetite for just about anything that grows and can do untold amounts of damage. Young and small plants are devoured to ground level, or neatly pruned down to a few inches with teeth of a precision that would put many secateurs to shame. Older, woody plants receive a different treatment, the bark being stripped as far as it is possible to reach. Once the bark is removed in an entire ring, the branch, or tree, if it has a single trunk, usually dies.

Several sizes up from the rabbit is the deer, which does a similar job, only on a larger scale, and it can jump, so reaching parts other four-legged vandals fail to reach. Sheep are rather like deer in their *modus operandi,* but as they generally move about in flocks, like soccer hooligans, they manage to inflict damage on a much more widespread scale. Cows and horses work at a higher level, and make an excellent job of pollarding young trees, especially those you do not want pollarded.

Human vandals, annoying as they are, are in the main easier to deal with than four-legged ones, as they are more easily deterred. Where large areas are involved, like public landscaping projects, often the sheer size of the task facing the desecrator will overwhelm him if there are enough plants and they are placed close enough together. The few that he does manage to get his hands on and destroy are barely noticeable amongst vast stretches of dense planting. Vandals with two legs also tend to be cowardly when it comes to pain, and if they should have the good luck to grasp firmly a well-developed specimen of, say, *Berberis julianae,* it is unlikely that they will do it again with that species, or anything that looks remotely like it.

Plants which are to be used in areas of high risk, whether from bored people, rabbits, sheep, deer, cows or whatever, should have the attribute of being capable of making a quick recovery. If the attacks are isolated or infrequent, therefore, the plants will get over them and eventually look reasonable again. Also, plants which snap off cleanly are more desirable than those which partially break and split.

Where rabbits are a problem, the most effective solution, though one which is very laborious and costly, is to forget about which plants are least palatable to the little horrors and fence the whole area with small-mesh wire netting, which should be high enough for them to be unable to reach any plants close to it, even while standing on their back legs and supporting themselves on the wire. Hares can be as bad, and are quite a lot taller. As most people know, rabbits can also burrow, so the netting must be buried to a depth of about 2 feet (60 cm) to prevent them getting underneath it.

Where this is impossible, the only other reliable answer is to net off groups of plants in a similar way – for example, a whole shrubbery or herbaceous border. This does not look particularly good, so you may find it better to abandon all thoughts of smaller subjects and aim instead for grass and trees with a single trunk, the base of which should be protected with a plastic rabbit guard – or two, even, as rabbits can reach upwards quite a long way. A more recent development of this idea is the 'grow-tube', a translucent plastic tube wide enough to encase a small tree or shrub but too narrow for a rabbit to get at the contents. This has the additional benefit of acting like a mini-greenhouse, offering protection from the weather as well as animals until the plant is big enough to pop out at the top, when it is usually able to take care of itself.

There are many species which will grow fairly well from the base if they get the chance, and these are the only remaining hope for anyone with a rabbit problem who cannot use any of the above

Eschscholzia californica (top) and *Linum grandiflorum* will flower well in very
shallow soil

Berberis stenophylla (top left, overleaf) quickly forms a vandal-proof hedge
Berberis thunbergii 'Silver Beauty' *(top right, overleaf)* is very prickly
Rosa rugosa 'Frau Dagmar Hastrup' *(overleaf)* will deter vandals

methods. These will be listed and described in detail shortly.

Larger animals are even more difficult to deal with. A garden known to be invaded by deer from time to time really should be fenced properly to keep them out, as even if the damage is only occasional, it can permanently ruin the shape of a good tree or shrub. Deer fencing must be tall enough to stop them jumping over, but they do not burrow, so it need not be sunk into the ground.

Farm animals and horses can be extremely destructive, and every precaution should be taken to prevent their access before the area is planted – I have so often seen literal examples of 'shutting the stable door after the horse has bolted'. They like both bark and young shoots; again, the removal of too much bark will seriously weaken the plant and often causes eventual death. Stout – and usually expensive – fencing is the only real answer here, preferably of strong timber or iron, so it cannot be 'bulldozed' down. Cattle and horses have long necks, so the space between the fence and any reachable plants must be adequate.

Of course, if there is a mature hedge around the animals, so much the better. It does not really matter what it comprises, the old mixed hedge is ideal, and quickthorn, blackthorn, field maple and the like are excellent as these have the capacity to regrow quickly if cut back, either intentionally or accidentally. They can also be 'laid' - that is, the trunks are partially severed so they can be bent over at an angle, supported by a framework of flexible wooden rods; this makes an impenetrable base and thick new growth. This job is a very skilled one and best left to an experienced craftsman; one can generally be found by contacting the local branch of CoSIRA or the Agricultural Training Board.

Really mature trees are not under as much threat from rabbits and farm animals as the bark and wood is too tough. Animals will feed off any younger material which should happen to be within their reach,

Clematis 'Comtesse de Bouchard' (*top left, previous page*) will flower on a north or east fence or wall

Kerria japonica 'Pleniflora' (*top right, previous page*) can be trained against north and east wall and fences

Clematis 'William Kennett' (*previous page*) flowers in shade

Hippophae rhamnoides (*top*) and Limonium (statice) are not damaged by salt in the air or soil

but this can lend a charm of its own to a larger area – most of us are familiar with the 'pruned-off' effect of cattle eating the lower growth of large parkland trees.

Goat-keeping has become very popular in recent years, and goats are perhaps the most destructive of all common farm animals, as they will chomp their way through most things of vegetable or mineral origin. It is extremely important, therefore, that any planted area close to goats should be strongly fenced; goats can stand on their back legs, too, so the barrier must be tall enough.

While thinking about vandals, we must not forget the family puppy, which can do untold amounts of damage to a garden. Correct training is the theoretical, though not always practical, answer, as I know from past bitter experience. The alternative of choosing thorny plants, and those which will regrow quickly, is the only workable alternative if you are not to put the garden out-of-bounds, with the hope that this is just a passing phase. I have had dogs for many years, and am now firmly of the opinion that the perfect garden and the average dog cannot exist together, but making sure you spend enough time with the animal to prevent it getting bored is essential.

A final word of caution: there are a few plants which are toxic in varying degrees to higher animals, and therefore where there is a known risk of farm livestock gaining access to an area, these should be avoided. The worst is yew which is almost invariably fatal. Rhododendrons, eaten in sufficient quantity, can have the same effect, and laurel also should not be planted.

Spiny plants likely to have a deterrent effect

All **berberis** have unpleasant prickles, so it does not matter which you choose; they are all nasty to handle. The most effective hedging berberis is *B. stenophylla,* which has scented, warm, yellow flowers in late spring, is evergreen, and produces suckers which quickly form an impassable barrier. Nearly as effective as a hedge are the various forms of *B. thunbergii,* which are deciduous, but produce berries which attract small birds and colour well in the autumn. There are several purple-leaved cultivars, like 'Atropurpurea', ottawensis 'Superba', 'Helmond Pillar', 'Red Chief' and 'Rose Glow'. 'Green Carpet' is a useful spreading form where ground cover is needed.

Of the other evergreen varieties, I find *B. julianae* a most attractive, medium-sized shrub as its largish leaves turn red in the autumn. In my own 'front garden' (more of a front than a garden!) it is the only plant, apart from pyracantha, which doesn't receive late-night attention from home-going revellers. *B. gagnepainii,* and its hybrid 'Wallichiana Purpurea', have long, narrow, crinkled leaves and an upright habit, which makes them useful in tight spaces. 'Wallich's Purple' has blue-green undersides to the leaves and the young growths have a purple sheen. I made the mistake of buying *B. media* 'Parkjeweel' a few years ago to include in a bed of small shrubs; in my garden it grows much larger than its suggested 3 feet (1 metre) spread, and makes the job of tidying the area very painful, but it does have pleasant yellow flowers and good autumn colour, and if you really want to give someone agony, I can fully recommend it.

Cortaderia (pampas grass) (see page 60) does not have thorns as such, but very sharp, slightly barbed edges to its long, grass-like leaves which are capable of inflicting a deep cut. Nobody in his right mind would attempt to pull one up without thick gloves, but four-legged vandals are much more tolerant of the inconvenience it can cause.

Pampas grass

The best varieties of **crataegus** (hawthorn) are described on page 43. Multi-branched shrubs are less likely to be permanently affected by damage than standards trained on a single trunk. These will regrow lower down, but the standard shape will be spoilt, so it is not worth spending the extra money on this form in the first place.

Elaeagnus angustifolia (oleaster) is a very spiny shrub with silvery-grey foliage and fragrant flowers in June.

Hippophae rhamnoides (sea buckthorn) – see page 120) would make a good hedge for a spot likely to come under attack from human vandals, and judging by the proliferation of growth on the rabbit-infested dunes of north Lincolnshire, it will eventually defeat these pests too.

Pyracantha are described more fully on pages 98–99. It is advisable to obtain well-grown plants as their spines are more fully developed. Mature pyracanthas recover well from damage if the affected areas are tidied up with a sharp knife or secateurs to prevent rotting.

Most **roses** have thorns that make handling difficult, although they seem to cause no problems for farm animals, especially sheep and deer. *Rosa rugosa* also produces suckers and is invariably grown on its own rootstock, so one or two accidental 'hard prunings' will not affect healthy plants much, as they will regenerate from the base. In addition, the thorns, though not long and hard, are profuse and have the irritating habit of embedding themselves firmly in the fleshy part of the hand, where they remain quite happily until the area turns septic. *R. rugosa* is a pleasant plant otherwise, with magenta or white flowers throughout summer, followed by large, red hips which, if the birds will let you, can be made into rose-hip jelly. Additionally, the leaves turn a bright, clear yellow, before falling in the autumn.

Ulex (gorse – see page 61) is likely to be nibbled in its youth, but if you can manage to establish it most vandals usually avoid it (goats excepting!).

Mature **yuccas** (see page 66) have very hard, leathery leaves which are difficult to harm; they are sword-like in shape and have a sharp point on the end, which can give one a nasty jab if not careful.

Shrubs capable of regrowing quickly or breaking cleanly
Both *Buddleia davidii*, the butterfly bush, and *B. globosa*, which has orange, ball-shaped flowers, are capable of growing again from the base if cut down, and so will recover from a 'one-off' attack. Young plants, of course, can be uprooted, so are still vulnerable.

Cornus alba and *sanguinea* produce coloured stems which will come from the base if the whole plant is cut down. In addition, the young stems are very flexible and so do not snap off easily, although they can be eaten.

In a way, **Corylus avellana** (hazel) rather fits into the same category as cornus, in as much as mature plants can be cut hard back

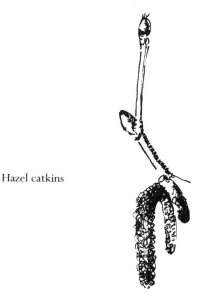

Hazel catkins

and will come up again happily, producing an ever-thickening mass of young growth from the base. If you are wanting nuts, however, it is not recommended that the bush is pruned hard back too regularly.

Many of the prostrate varieties of **cotoneaster**, like *C. dammeri,* root where they touch, and so once established are very difficult to pull out. Unfortunately animals, particularly rabbits, find the young plants delicious, and so it is almost impossible to establish them without providing protection while they are getting a foothold. The low-growing, evergreen forms of *euonymus* are similar; get them going and they will stand up to rough handling fairly well, but newly planted subjects will vanish overnight through the actions of a variety of vandals.

Eleagnus ebbingei and *E. commutata* will regrow from lower down if damaged. *E. commutata* is a nice-looking shrub with silver leaves and small, scented flowers in May.

Heathers will stand nibbling by small animals and really old bushes can tolerate periodic cropping by larger ones, but they do not

135

like being uprooted and thrown over a neighbour's hedge.

Forsythia is invaluable as a quick-growing garden shrub. There are some good new smaller cultivars, but these are not suitable for planting where rapid regrowth is wanted. *Forsythia* 'Lynwood' is still perhaps the best variety; it can get too big for many modern gardens but it will re-establish well if subjected to damage. It has extremely large, yellow flowers in profusion in early spring, but the more you cut the shrub back, the more green growth it will produce at the expense of flowers.

Other shrubs in the same category are ***Ribes sanguineum*** (flowering currant) and the more rapid-growing forms of **philadelphus** (mock orange), especially 'Virginal', with its profusion of

Flowering currant

heavily scented, pure white flowers in June.

Ivies, planted as ground cover, are virtually impossible to remove once established. Most strong-growing varieties are suitable – for really tough ground cover, *Hedera colchica* (Persian ivy) and *H. helix* 'Hibernica' (Irish ivy) are perhaps most suitable.

The same applies to ***Hypericum calycinum*** (rose of Sharon) – get it growing and it will run all over the place, but in the right spot, the big yellow flowers and low growth habit can be most useful. If you have rabbits and the covering is getting out of hand, they will do a very skilful pruning job for you.

Holly has two main attributes as far as vandalism is concerned. The first is that many varieties, though not all, have prickly leaves – if you want a really wicked one, plant the hedgehog holly (*Ilex aquifolium* 'Ferox'). The other is that even fairly young plants have a marvellous capacity for recovery, as I discovered earlier this year when mine was savaged by a careless thatcher, who, having broken it down by dumping bales of reed on it – and anyone who has survived the experience of being re-thatched will know that these bales are only liftable with the aid of a hoist! – proceeded to bury it in rubbish for several months. My poor *Ilex aquifolium argenteo-marginata* (silver holly) looked fit for less than compost when it was finally rescued, but some weeks after cutting it right back, new growth started to appear, and although the shape will never be the same again, it is not altogether lost.

Kerria japonica produces green, stem-like branches which do not snap easily and will quickly come up again from the base. It makes large bushes in time through the production of suckers. The flowers are yellow, mainly produced in the spring, but sometimes there is a lesser flush in autumn. *Leycesteria formosa*, the flowering nutmeg, also has suckering, green stems, with claret-coloured bracts and purple berries in autumn, which will attract birds into the garden. It is often planted as pheasant cover, as is that other indestructable plant, *Lonicera pileata*, which can be virtually demolished and still come up smiling.

Ligustrum (privet), especially *L. ovalifolium* and its golden-leaved form, can be sawn off at the base and still survive, so makes a useful hedge if you think it is possible that someone sometime might drive a car uninvited into your front garden.

Mahonia aquifolium (Oregon grape), an evergreen, medium-growing shrub with yellow flowers in spring, is also a sucker-producer, and so cannot be easily be pulled out after a year or two of growth. It can become straggly and untidy in a garden situation after a while, and benefits from periodic cutting back if you have not got a friendly animal who will do the job for you. The berries will attract wildlife, and are edible, though not particularly palatable.

Potentilla twigs are difficult to snap off and the bushes will stand some nibbling. (See page 63.)

The **ornamental blackberries** are not as prickly as their fruiting relatives, but all produce strong-growing stems. For low-growing ground cover, you cannot beat *Rubus tricolor,* as not only does it grow strongly, it also roots along the prostrate stems, so even if parts of it are pulled out, it is unlikely that the whole covering will be removed. Two white-stemmed forms, *R. cockburnianus* and *R. thibetanus,* are particularly ornamental.

As I have mentioned on page 27, **willows**, except dwarf varieties, need to be planted with care, but as most of them will grow again from the root, they are worth considering where space is not a problem, but damage of one sort and another is.

The most vandal-proof, invasive forms of **symphoricarpos** (snowberry) like *S. albus, S. laevigatus* and *S. chenaultii* 'Hancock' are not really suitable for modern gardens, but could be considered for real problem areas, as it is difficult to kill them. The *S. doorenbosii* hybrids are non-suckering and by no means indestructible, but will stand a certain amount of 'humpy' after a year or two's growth. 'Magic Berry' (carmine berries), 'Mother of Pearl' (white, tinted pink), and 'White Hedge' will all make good screens for areas where damage could occur, providing they are given a little time to take a foothold.

Common elder (sambucus) is extremely hard to remove once it is established, and in a wild area it is worth considering, as it will certainly regrow after animal damage. The coloured-leaved forms 'Albo-variegata' (white edges), 'Aurea' (golden leaves), 'Aureomarginata' (yellow edges), and 'Purpurea' (leaves flushed purple), are more useful for the majority of gardens; although they are not as strong-growing, they have good powers of recuperation.

Spiraea × *bumalda* **'Anthony Waterer'** is a pretty, if once over-planted, small shrub with twiggy stems and reddish flower heads in high summer. It can actually benefit from a periodic slaughtering to encourage the production of young shoots from the base.

Some **viburnum** species are too exacting to take kindly to a hammering, but the guelder rose, *Viburnum opulus,* the native wayfaring tree, *Viburnum lanata,* and *Viburnum rhytidophyllum,* which has thick, heavily veined, evergreen leaves and dirty white flowers in June, followed by red berries, will recover if damaged.

The **periwinkle** (vinca) survives adverse conditions as far as vandalism is concerned in a similar manner to *Rubus tricolor* in that the stems root at every node (leaf joint) if they are in contact with the soil and so it is a difficult plant to eradicate entirely. (For the best varieties see pages 49–50.)

Like forsythia, philadelphus and ribes, **weigela** will survive moderate amounts of damage by being able to regenerate reasonably quickly. The variegated forms of the plant, and the newer, dwarf cultivars are unsuitable for planting in areas liable to attack from animals or over-oiled Saturday-nighters, but taller hybrids such as 'Abel Carriere' (carmine flowers with a yellow throat), 'Bristol Ruby' and 'Newport Red' are all tough enough to fight off damage providing it is not too severe and the bushes are given some time to establish.

Postscript

There may be some people who have read this book hoping to find excuses for abandoning all efforts where their land is less than perfect. They will have found few words of comfort in these pages.

Making the best of a bad job is a state of mind. If you look on a garden with problem areas as a disaster, it will quickly become one. On the other hand, if a difficult spot is viewed as positively a challenge and a blessing, then given a little thought and a bit of hard work, something special will soon emerge. Gardening under good conditions can be fun, but to produce good results from adversity is definitely worth boasting about, and at the very least your garden will be unique.

Useful addresses
and Bibliography

Nurseries

Notcutts' Nurseries, Woodbridge, Suffolk: wide range of all types of plants. Also have garden centres at Nuneham Courtney, Bagshot, Maidstone, St. Albans, Peterborough, Ardleigh, Norwich and Solihull, where postal orders may be collected.

Bressingham Gardens, Diss, Norfolk: specialists in alpines, dwarf conifers, shrubs for modern gardens, heathers and herbaceous plants for collection at the plant centre or by mail order.

Hillier Nurseries (Winchester), Ltd., Ampfield House, Ampfield, Romsey, Hampshire: very wide range of all types of plants including many unusual varieties.

Hillier Nurseries (Winchester), Ltd, Ampfield House, Ampfield, Sunningdale, Winchester, Ampfield.

Wildmore Water Gardens, New York, Coningsby, Lincoln: aquatic and moisture-loving plants.

Specialist clubs and organizations

British Pteridological (Fern) Society, 42 Lewisham Road, Smethwick, Warley, West Midlands.

Hardy Plant Soceity, 10 St Barnabas Road, Emmer Green, Caversham, Reading, Berks.

British Hosta and Hemerocallis Society, 42 Fairoak Drive, Eltham, London SE9.

Seed companies willing to give advice on maritime wild flowers

Johnsons Seeds, London Road, Boston, Lincs.

John Chambers, 15 Westleigh Road, Barton Seagrave, Kettering, Northants.

Suggested further reading

Guide to the Specialist Nurseries and Garden Suppliers of Britain and Ireland, edited by Sarah Cotton, Garden Art Press.
The Dry Garden, Beth Chatto, Dent.
The Damp Garden, Beth Chatto, Dent.
Hillier's Manual of Trees and Shrubs, David and Charles.
The Flower Expert, Dr D Hessayon, pbi Publications.
At the Water's Edge – Gardening with Moisture Loving Plants, Philip Swindells, Ward Lock.
Plants for Shade, Allen Paterson, Dent.
Plants for Small Gardens, Geoffrey K Coombes, Cassells (Wisley Handbook Series).
Fisk's Clematis Nursery Catalogue, 65p, including postage from Fisk's Clematis Nursery, Westleton, Saxmundham, Suffolk. A comprehensive booklet dealing with planting, training, maintenance and problems of clematis, with a list of most of the species and varieties available at present, well illustrated with colour photographs.
Clematis, Ethne Reuss Clarke, Collins Aura Handbooks.
The Hardy Plant Society's New Plant Directory, Chris Phillips, Moorland Publishing.